THE CENTERS OF CIVILIZATION SERIES

140-8669

(*Complete List on Page 189*)

Istanbul

AND THE
CIVILIZATION
OF THE
OTTOMAN EMPIRE

AND THE CIVILIZATION OF THE OTTOMAN EMPIRE

by Bernard Lewis

NORMAN : UNIVERSITY OF OKLAHOMA PRESS

Library of Congress Catalog Card Number: 63-17161

Copyright © 1963 by the University of Oklahoma Press, Norman, Publishing
Division of the University. Manufactured in the U.S.A. First edition, 1963;
second printing, 1968; third printing, 1972; fourth printing, 1978; fifth
printing, 1982.

Istanbul and the Civilization of the Ottoman Empire is Volume 9 in The
Centers of Civilization Series.

To Ruth

Preface

THE GREAT CITY by the Bosporus has been known by many names. To the Slavs, it was Tsargrad, the Emperor's city; to the Northmen, Myklagaard or Micklegarth, the Great Town. The Greeks and Romans knew it as Byzantium, the name of the old settlement on the site; as new Rome, and above all as Constantinupolis, the city of Constantine, who founded his new imperial capital there in 330 A.D. The new name, in the forms Kostantiniyya or Kustantiniyya, was also used by the Muslims beyond the eastern and southern borders of the Empire.

Most commonly, the Byzantines were content to speak of their magnificent capital simply as "the city," *hê polis*. It is this word that probably underlies another name, attested in Muslim historical and geographical writings as early as the tenth century. The name Istanbul is of disputed etymology: the explanation most generally accepted derives it from the phrase *eis tên polin,* to the city, which the Muslims might have heard from their Greek neighbors in Asia Minor. Though widely used by Turks and other Muslims, the name Istanbul did not pass into Ottoman official usage. An imaginative adaptation of it, *Islambol,* full of Islam, appeared for a while on Ottoman coins and documents; but for the most part the Ottoman Sultans, from the conquest until the fall of the Empire, preferred to retain the name Kostantiniyya and to vary it with such poetic designations as the Abode of Sovereignty and the Threshold of Bliss. The final and official replacement of Constantinople by Istanbul did not take place until 1930.

For many centuries, however, Istanbul has been the common designation given by the Turks to the great city which they conquered and made the center of their empire and civilization. In the following pages an attempt is made to portray some aspects of this empire and civilization, as they flourished in the days of Ottoman greatness. As far as possible this has been done in the words of contemporary Turkish and Western observers.

The extract from Kâtib Chelebi in Chapter VI is in the version of Dr. G. L. Lewis; my thanks are due to him and to Messrs. George Allen and Unwin for permission to reproduce it. The passages from Sad el-Din in Chapter I and from Evliya Chelebi in Chapter V are in the translations of E. J. W. Gibb and J. Hammer, respectively, both slightly revised; the poem by Mesihi in Chapter VI is in the version of Sir William Jones. Passages from continental European writers have been cited in contemporary or nearly contemporary English translations. Other English versions of Turkish texts are my

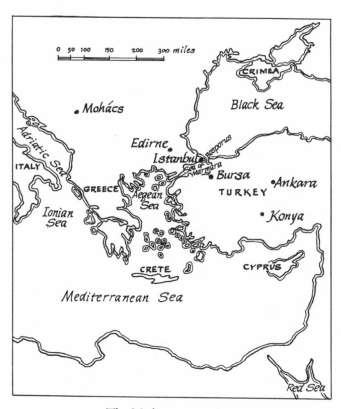

The Mediterranean Area

own. My thanks are due to the editor of *Islamic Studies,* Karachi, for permission to reproduce some of my translations of Lutfi Pasha, Kochu Bey, and Kâtib Chelebi, which were originally published in the first issue of that journal, in March, 1962.

I should like to express my gratitude to Professor A. T. Hatto and Dr. V. L. Ménage, both of the University of London, who read through my typescript and made many suggestions for its improvement. My general debt to the masters of Ottoman studies, and particularly to Professor Paul Wittek, will be obvious to all workers in that field.

Bernard Lewis

LONDON, ENGLAND

Contents

Istanbul

AND THE
CIVILIZATION
OF THE
OTTOMAN EMPIRE

I. The Conquest

ON TUESDAY, MAY 29, 1453, in the early hours of the morning, the vast armies encamped outside the walls of Constantinople launched their final general assault. A hundred years had passed since the Turks had crossed the Dardanelles from Asia and won their first foothold in Europe, in the Gallipoli Peninsula; more than fifty since their Sultan Bayezid, master of the Balkans, had first tried to capture the Imperial city. On that occasion, Constantinople had been saved by intervention from the West and distraction from the East. In 1410 and 1422 other Turkish rulers, Prince Musa and Sultan Murad, had laid siege to the city, but again were interrupted and deflected from their purpose. Now, a new and young Sultan, Mehemmed, known to history as the Conqueror, had begun the last and greatest siege. From the broad lands that he ruled in Europe and Asia, he had brought a great army to the walls of Constantinople, to capture the Imperial capital and add it, as coping stone, to the Empire that his fathers had conquered.

Of the once great empire over which the Byzantine Emperors had ruled, only the city remained, with a few scattered outposts in Greece, too far and too poor to offer much help. Of the once great and teeming city, only a remnant survived, shrunken and depleted, with a population of barely fifty thousand. There were grass-grown ruins and empty fields within the city walls; but the mighty triple land-walls still stood, and behind them the last legions of the Roman Empire prepared to defend their capital.

They were not many; the chroniclers put them at about eight thousand men, including nearly three thousand Italian volunteers, to hold four miles of land-walls, and to guard the approaches from the sea. They were helped by a small fleet in the Golden Horn, protected by a boom from the Turkish navy outside. Against them were massed the armies of an empire that extended from the Danube to the upper Euphrates, from the Adriatic to the Black Sea. The regular Janissary infantry, the feudal *Sipahi* cavalry, and a great force of artillery, with guns of terrifying size to batter the millennial walls of the city—all these, with the numberless volunteers, skirmishers, and auxiliaries made up a force that has been estimated at from 100,000 to 150,000 men; a fleet of several hundred war vessels patrolled the Bosporus, and in one night the Sultan succeeded in transporting seventy or eighty warships overland, on wooden runners, across Galata and launched them in the upper part of the Golden Horn, thus investing the triangular-shaped city on all three sides.

The siege had already lasted for seven weeks. On April 7, the Sultan's armies had taken up their positions along the whole length of the land-walls, from Marmara to the Golden

Horn; on the eleventh they placed their guns in position against the walls; on the twelfth they began their bombardment, which continued for the next six weeks, battering and destroying the walls of the city; on the twenty-first they moved their fleet across the hills behind Galata into the Golden Horn. The first Turkish assault against the walls was launched on April 18; other attacks followed, by land and by sea, but all were repelled by the indomitable defenders. At a council held in the Turkish camp on May 26 or 27, the venerable Grand Vizier, Halil Pasha, urged the abandonment of the enterprise which he had opposed from the start, and no doubt there were others to support him. But the Sultan—young and ambitious, and resentful of the elderly advisers left to him by his father—decided otherwise. On Sunday, May 27, he conferred with his commanders, visited his troops, and sent his heralds through the camp to proclaim that if his soldiers stormed the walls and captured the city, it would be theirs for three days, to sack and pillage without restraint or impediment. Monday, May 28, was passed in preparation, and on Tuesday morning, an hour or two after midnight, the signal was given for the general assault.

The first attack was launched by an expendable rabble of irregulars and adventurers, many of them of European origin; they advanced to the walls, but were driven back with heavy losses, having achieved the Sultan's purposes of tiring the defenders and draining their ammunition. The second assault, more serious, was made by the crack Anatolian divisions—armored, disciplined soldiers, who still failed to breach the defenses, and were forced to withdraw. Finally, in the early light of dawn, the Sultan sent in his élite troops—his bodyguard, his archers and lancers, and the twelve thousand men of the corps of Janissaries.

The first of them to gain a foothold on the wall was a giant Janissary called Hasan. He was felled by a stone, overpowered, and killed; but others followed him and forced their way to the inner side of the stockades. Meanwhile other Turks had entered the city through the neglected Circus Gate, and within fifteen minutes tens of thousands of them had penetrated the defenses. Among the anguished and exhausted Greeks the cry arose, *"Healô hê polis*—the city is captured; the Turkish flags are flying on the towers." The attackers, from every side, swarmed over the broken walls to overwhelm the surviving defenders and begin the sack of the conquered city. In the final desperate struggle, Constantine XI Palaeologus Dragases, last of the Emperors, died sword in hand defending his lost capital, "the empire as his winding-sheet."

Some hours later, the Sultan himself entered the city, riding on horseback through the gate now called Topkapi, with an escort of high dignitaries and a Janissary guard. He rode to the great Church of the Holy Wisdom—Hagia Sophia—where he dismounted and entered. There he summoned an Imam, who went up into the pulpit and intoned the Muslim creed: "I testify that there is no God but God. I testify that our lord Muhammad is the Prophet of God." The Greek cathedral had become a Turkish mosque. In place of the Emperor in Constantinople, the Sultan reigned in Istanbul—once again to burgeon and flower as the center of a vast empire and a great civilization.

A vivid picture of the wonderment of the Turks at the

splendors they had conquered is drawn by Tursun Beg, a veteran of the conquest, secretary to the Sultan's council, and one of the first Ottoman writers of literary prose. In his biography of Mehemmed the Conqueror, written towards the end of the fifteenth century, he describes the Sultan's entry into the city:

> The great ones of the state and the attendants of the Presence caused the gates of the city to be opened . . . and the Sultan, Mehemmed Gazi, with his scholars and his commanders, deigned to enter . . . while the congregation of angels in heaven uttered praises, and caused the sound of the verse "These are the gardens of Eden: enter them endowed with eternal life" to reach the ears of mortal men. First he went about, gazing upon the storeyed houses and markets of this broad and ancient city, and then expressed a desire to see the church called Aya Sofya, which is a sign from Paradise:
>
> > If you seek Paradise, Oh you Sufi,
> > The topmost heaven is Aya Sofya.

Tursun goes on to say that, despite its great strength and peerless beauty, the church had suffered from the ravages of time, and some of the subordinate buildings of the complex had fallen in ruin. But the great Dome still stood:

> What a dome, that vies in rank with the nine spheres of heaven! In this work a perfect master displayed the whole of the architectural science. With half-domes one upon the other, with angles both acute and obtuse, with peerless vaults, like the arched brows of heart-ravishing girls, with stalactite adornments, he made the interior so vast, that it can hold 50,000 people. . . . The Emperor of the World, having looked upon the strange and wondrous images and adornments that were

7

on the concave inner surface, deigned to climb up to the convex outer surface, mounting as [Jesus] the spirit of God ascended to the fourth sphere of heaven. Looking down as he passed, from the battlements at each level, on to the marbled court below, he went up to the dome. When he saw the dependent buildings of this mighty structure fallen in ruin, he thought of the impermanence and instability of this world, and of its ultimate destruction. In sadness, a verse of his sweetness-diffusing utterance reached my humble ear, and remained engraved on the tablet of my heart:

> The spider is curtain-bearer in the Palace of Chosroes
> The owl sounds the relief in the castle of Afrasiyab.

While the Sultan indulged his melancholy reflections on the mutability of human glories, the conquering soldiery enjoyed the simpler delights of victory. Some idea of their outlook may be obtained from another and very different Turkish writer of the time, the chronicler Ashikpashazade, whose narrative, written in plain Turkish for plain men, is close to the views of the Turkish *gazis,* or frontier fighters:

> For fifty days the battle went on by day and night. On the fifty-first day the Sultan ordered free plunder. They attacked. On the fifty-first day, a Tuesday, the fortress was captured. There was good booty and plunder. Gold and silver and jewels and fine stuffs were brought and stacked in the camp market. They began to sell them. They made the people of the city slaves and killed their emperor, and the *gazis* embraced their pretty girls. . . . On the first Friday after the conquest they recited the communal prayer in Aya Sofya, and the Islamic invocation was read in the name of Sultan Mehemmed Khan Gazi. . . .

More than a century later, one of the most famous of Ottoman historians, Sa'd ed-Din, ended his long and literary narrative of the conquest with these ecstatic words:

> That wide region, that strong and lofty city . . . from being the nest of the owl of error, was turned into the capital of glory and honor. Through the noble efforts of the Muhammedan sultan, for the evil-voiced clash of the bells of the shameless misbelievers was substituted the Muslim call to prayer, the sweet five-times repeated chant of the Faith of glorious rites, and the ears of the people of the Holy War were filled with the melody of the call to prayer. The churches which were within the city were emptied of their vile idols, and cleansed from their filthy and idolatrous impurities; and by the defacement of their images, and the erection of the Islamic prayer niches and pulpits, many monasteries and chapels became the envy of the Gardens of Paradise. The temples of the misbelievers were turned into the mosques of the pious, and the rays of the light of Islam drove away the hosts of darkness from that place so long the abode of the despicable infidels, and the streaks of the dawn of the Faith dispelled the lurid blackness of oppression, for the word, irresistible as destiny, of the fortunate sultan became supreme in the governance of this new dominion. . .

The last bastion of Christendom in Southeastern Europe had fallen; a new power was established, which an Elizabethan clergyman, writing a century and a half later, called "the glorious Empire of the Turks, the present Terror of the World."

II. The Conquerors

THE NAME TURK appears in history for the first time in the sixth century A.D., when Chinese annals speak of a powerful empire in Central Asia founded by a people called the *Tu Kiu.* No doubt, peoples of Turkish stock played a role of some importance in more ancient times, in the history of Asia and even of Europe. But the Tu Kiu—easily recognizable as Turks—are the first among the Turkish peoples to appear in history under the name that later came to be distinctively theirs. This empire, which stretched across the steppe country from the border of China to the Black Sea, attracted the attention of Greek as well as Chinese historians; it was however of short duration and soon broke up into warring fragments, some of which fell under Chinese domination. These early Central Asian Turks were no mere barbarians. They already possessed a written language, and important groups among them were affected by the religions of the civilized world, including Buddhism, Manichaeism, and Nestorian Christianity.

It was, however, none of these that the Turkish peoples finally adopted. In the course of the eighth century, the Arabs, who had already triumphantly carried the new faith of Islam across Persia from Arabia, conquered and occupied the lands between the Oxus and the Jaxartes, and came into direct contact with the Turkish peoples of inner Asia. From this time on the Turks, though never conquered by the Muslims, came increasingly under their influence. Frontier fighters and dervish missionaries, most of them of Turkish origin, combined to carry the new faith to the unsubdued tribes beyond the Islamic imperial frontier. In time, most of the Turkish peoples accepted the Muslim faith; with it they adopted the Arabic script and much of the rich and complex civilization of classical Islam.

From the early ninth century the caliphs of Islam began to import Turkish slaves from the eastern border, chiefly for service as soldiers. These slaves were known as *mamluk*—an Arabic word meaning "owned"—to distinguish them from the humble slaves used for domestic or economic purposes. The Turkish *mamluks,* though nominally of servile status, actually came to form a privileged military caste, recruited by capture and purchase, but held together by strong regimental loyalties. In time they came to form the main core of the armies of Islam. Commanders easily became governors, and governors soon founded dynasties. The first Turkish rulers in Islam appear already in the ninth century. By the eleventh century there were few rulers who were not Turks. As the armies of Islam became more Turkish, and the governments of Islam more military, the Turks established a domination in the lands of Islam that lasted for a thousand years.

Meanwhile a movement was in preparation that was to bring the Turks right across to the Mediterranean and beyond —and in so doing to transform the Middle East and Eastern Europe. The great migration of the steppe peoples into the Middle East began in the tenth century with obscure convulsions in the remote lands to the north, which drove the Oguz group of Turkish tribes southward across the Jaxartes into Islamic territory. This was the first of a series of waves of invasion and migration from the steppe that did not end until the fifteenth century.

In the establishment of Turkish power and the spread of Turkish peoples and customs in the lands of Islam, two periods are particularly significant. The first is that of the Seljuk Great Sultans, who ruled the Middle East for about a century, from their conquest of Baghdad in 1055 to the death of Sultan Sanjar in 1157. The second was that of the Mongol conquests in the thirteenth century, and the period of Mongol supremacy and influence that followed it.

The Seljuks were not a tribe, still less a nation. They were a family of Oguz Turks claiming descent from a certain Seljuk ibn Dukak, and appear to have entered the Islamic lands in the late tenth century and settled in the neighborhood of Bukhara, where they became Muslims. The sons of Seljuk became professional *condottieri,* with their own war bands, and served in the armies of various Muslim states. Finally they began to operate on their own account, and were soon able to wield great power and win vast lands. The grandsons of Seljuk overran eastern Persia, and then turned westward, conquering as they went, until in 1055 one of them, Tugrul Beg, led his army into the imperial city of Baghdad. A new

empire had arisen in Islam, known as that of the Great Seljuks. From Iraq, the Seljuks continued their advance westward. One wave of invaders advanced into Syria and Pales-
tine, which they wrested from local and Egyptian rulers;
another overflowed into Anatolia, then still part of the Byzantine Empire. The way was prepared for them by the decisive
battle of Manzikert in Armenia where the Seljuk Sultan, Alp
Arslan, inflicted a crushing defeat on the Byzantine Emperor,
Romanus IV Diogenes. The Turkish invaders, succeeding
where all previous Muslim attackers had failed, pushed the
frontier of Greek Christendom back to western Anatolia, and
incorporated this new and rich territory in the world of Islam.
In a crusading chronicle of 1190, the name "Turkey" appears
for the first time, appplied to the new Turkish lands in Asia
Minor. It became the common designation in Western,
though not in Turkish usage, for what became and remained
a Muslim, Turkish land.

At first the Seljuk Sultanate was in theory one and indivisible, with one great Sultan reigning over all the central
lands of Islam. But with the decline of the Great Seljuks, and
the breakup of their empire into a number of smaller states
ruled by Seljuk princes or officers, a new conception appears—
that of the territorial or regional sultanate.

One of the most important of the Seljuk successors states
was in central and eastern Anatolia. The conquest of Anatolia was fundamentally the work of migrating nomadic
tribes and of bands of *gazis,* accomplished without any delib-
erate intention or plan on the part of the Seljuk state. Once
the conquest was under way, however, a Seljuk prince, Süleyman ibn Kutulmush, was sent to organize the newly won

territories. While the march-warriors fought on and advanced the frontier against Christendom, the Seljuk officers came after them, setting up a regular Islamic administration. Within a century, Süleyman and his successors had built up a powerful Turkish state, with its capital in the ancient city of Iconium, which the Turks call Konya. This dynasty, which with varying success ruled Turkish Anatolia until the beginning of the fourteenth century, was known as the Sultans of Rum.

The name Rum is an Arabic echo of the mighty name of Rome, which, in the East as in the West, lingered in strange places long after the Roman Empire was dead. In Muslim usage of medieval times, the Rum were the Byzantines—the *Rhomaioi* who, from the new Rome by the Bosporus, ruled over the eastern remnant of the Roman Empire, and the Land of Rum was the territories over which they ruled. Not unnaturally, the terms came to be used more especially of the Asian provinces of the Empire, with which the Muslims had most contact.

It was therefore into the land of Rum that the Turkish invaders of the eleventh century came—and it was over the land and people of Rum that the Seljuk Sultans of Konya held sway. Before long the adjective Rumi was applied to the Turkish as well as the Greek inhabitants and was used to designate the Anatolian Turks in places as far away as Egypt and India.

The Seljuk Sultanate of Rum was an Islamic monarchy on classical lines, with deep roots in the older Islamic world. The political independence of the frontier warriors and tribesmen who had conquered and colonized the country was curbed by the power of a strong, centralized monarchy; their faith was subjected to the scrutiny and control of a hierarchy of professional men of religion. In Konya and the other cities of the Sultanate, an urban Muslim élite had grown up; administrators and men of letters, jurists and divines, merchants and artisans moved from east and south into the newly colonized territories, bringing with them the old, high civilization of classical Islam, impressing on the country the traditional patterns of Islamic society and polity. The affinities—often the origins—of these men were in the heartlands of old Islam, of which they felt themselves to be a part. They had little in common with the fierce warriors and adventurers of the border.

In the thirteenth century Turkish Anatolia, together with the rest of the Middle East, underwent the crushing impact of the Mongol conquest. After conquering Persia, the Mongol horsemen swept on to Mesopotamia and Anatolia; on June 26, 1243, near Köse Dağ in Eastern Turkey, a Mongol detachment overwhelmed the army of the Sultan of Rum. Though the Mongols raided and plundered far into central Anatolia, they did not actually subjugate the Sultanate of Rum, preferring to reduce it to a vassal state. They had, however, dealt it a blow from which it never recovered. After dragging out an attenuated existence for some fifty years, it finally disappeared at the beginning of the fourteenth century. Most of eastern and central Anatolia became subject to the Mongol Il-Khans in Persia, and was ruled either by Mongol governors or by Turkish vassals. After the death of the Il-Khan Abu Said in 1336, the Mongol dominions in the Middle East broke up, and a number of small principalities, ruled by Mongol or Turkish dynasties, appeared in Persia, Mesopotamia, and Anatolia.

In Anatolia, the collapse of the central state authority and the irruption into the country of new waves of Turkish nomadic migrants, fleeing before the Mongols, had led to a revival of the frontier, and a new westward advance against Byzantium, which brought the whole of western Anatolia under Muslim Turkish rule. The peninsula was divided between a number of rival principalities; the most powerful of them was Karaman, which held the old Seljuk capital of Konya, and tried to establish continuity with the Seljuk Sultanate. The most active principalities were those of the far west, along the shores of the Sea of Marmara and the Aegean, where they were engaged by land and sea in the Holy War for Islam against the infidel.

Among the principalities of march-warriors who shared in the new conquests was one known by the name of its first ruler, Osman, who is said to have reigned from 1299 to 1326. Its people were called after him, *Osmanli*, or, in the common European corruption of the name, Ottomans. They were to achieve great things. Though their principality was at first smaller and less powerful than others that were its rivals, their position in the far west, on the borders of the Byzantine province of Bithynia and of Constantinople, gave them greater tasks and greater opportunities, and attracted support and recruits from all over Anatolia. This was the border state par excellence, whose unremitting struggle against the Christian enemy offered the different and, to different minds, equally attractive choices of glory, booty, and martyrdom.

In 1301, Osman won a victory over the Byzantines at Baphaion—in Turkish Koyunhisar—which allowed him to extend his possessions considerably at Byzantine expense. Under his successor Orhan (1326–62) progress was more rapid. In 1326, soon after the accession of their new ruler, the Ottomans took the heavily fortified city of Brusa (in Turkish Bursa), which became the capital of their rapidly growing state; seizing Nicaea (Iznik) in 1331 and Nicomedia (Izmit) in 1337. By about 1340 they had taken practically all that had remained to the Byzantines in Asia Minor, apart from the coastal fortresses facing and adjoining Constantinople itself. For the moment there was nowhere else to go, and a period of consolidation followed, partly occupied in the absorption of the neighboring Anatolian emirate of Karasi, to the southwest, which brought the Ottomans to the Dardanelles and the Aegean coast.

But the dynamism of the Ottoman march-warriors, reinforced by the inflow from other parts of Anatolia, could not long be halted. In 1345, at the request of the Byzantine Emperor John VI Cantacuzenus, Ottoman forces crossed to Europe, to help him in his struggle against his rival John V Palaeologus. Their return to Asia Minor, laden with booty, brought welcome news of the tempting new lands beyond the narrow waters of the Bosporus and the Dardanelles.

In 1354 two events occurred which helped to prepare the Ottomans for their next adventure in Europe. The first was the capture of Ankara, the first old Muslim city in Asia to fall into their hands. In Muslim possession for some two and a half centuries, Ankara had been part of the Seljuk Sultanate, and enjoyed a high level of urban commerce, culture, and government. Its acquisition brought into the Ottoman camp men with knowledge, skills, and experience that were to be needed in the government of an empire.

Of more immediate importance was the occupation of Gallipoli—the first foothold of the Ottoman Turks in Europe. Conceded by the Byzantine Emperor to his Ottoman auxiliaries, it became the base for a series of expeditions of conquest in the Balkans. Under their third ruler, Murad I (1362–89), the Turks made rapid progress in Europe. In about 1361 they had conquered Adrianople (Edirne), a vital strongpoint on the road from Constantinople to the Danube, and two or three years later they seized Philipopolis (Filibe). Edirne now became Murad's European headquarters, from which he won a series of swift and crushing victories in Macedonia, Bulgaria, and Serbia, culminating in the great battle of Kosovo Polje—the field of blackbirds—on June 6, 1389, which sealed the end of Serb independence. The Serbian king, Lazar, and the Sultan both perished, but the Turkish victory was assured.

Each war of conquest in Europe was preceded by an expansion of the Anatolian base of Ottoman power—sometimes by military, sometimes by peaceful means. South of the Ottoman dominions in Asia lay the emirate of Germiyan; much of its territory, including its capital, Kütahya, came as a dowry with the emir's daughter, when she married the Ottoman prince, Bayezid. In Hamid, south of Germiyan, Murad was able to buy out the emir, thanks to the wealth he had won by his European conquests. In Teke, beyond Hamid, his successor resorted to force of arms.

The fourth Ottoman ruler, Bayezid I (1389–1402) known as Yildirim, the Thunderbolt, succeeded to wide lands both in Asia and in Europe, where the Ottoman position had been secured by the victory of Kossovo. Turning back to the east, he launched his armies against the remaining Turkish emirates in Anatolia; Karaman, the most powerful of them, succumbed in 1390; the rest were soon absorbed, and within a few years Ottoman rule extended over all Turkish Anatolia, southward to the Aegean and the Mediterranean coasts, eastward to Sivas, Kayseri, and the upper Euphrates.

Bayezid was now master of Asia Minor and Southeastern Europe—in fact of most of the territories of the Byzantine Empire, apart from its capital. It was during these years that, at the end of 1394, he turned to Cairo with an interesting and significant request.

The real rulers of Egypt at that time were the Mamluk Sultans, whose empire had been established in the thirteenth century. After the destruction of the Caliphate of Baghdad by the Mongols, they had installed a refugee member of the Caliph's family as puppet Caliph, and had since maintained a line of shadow-caliphs at their court, as nominal religious heads under the effective rule of the Mamluk Sultans.

It was to the nominal Caliph in Cairo that Bayezid Beg, prince of the borders, sent an embassy with gifts, to request a diploma of investiture with the title "Sultan of Rum." The Mamluk Sultan might have hesitated a long time before approving the grant of the imperial title to a powerful and rising neighbor. But the looming menace of Timur, a new conqueror in the East, had made the Mamluks and Ottomans temporary allies, and Bayezid was therefore duly granted the title for which he had asked, in a diploma signed by the Commander of the Faithful in Cairo.

When Bayezid proclaimed himself Sultan of Rum, he was

appealing to many historic memories. No longer a mere border chief, he was now the sovereign of an Islamic Empire in the Old World, an heir to the bygone but not forgotten glories of the Seljuk Sultans of Konya—perhaps even a claimant to the remoter heritage of those Christian Emperors who had once ruled over all the lands of Rum.

The transition, though resulting from the conquests by the march-warriors, was by no means unresisted by them. The men on the frontier deeply resented the transformation of their leader from a chief to a monarch; they resented, too, the restriction of their freedom by the growing authority of the state, and there are many indications, in the early Ottoman sources, of anger and discontent at the gradual introduction of the classical Islamic apparatus of government—particularly of its legal and fiscal provisions.

In 1395, having swiftly crushed an attack by the Prince of Wallachia and reaffirmed his power in the Balkans, the new Sultan of Rum began to blockade the great walled city of Constantinople. From this he was briefly distracted by a crusade of Western chivalry, on which he inflicted a crushing defeat at Nicopolis, by the Danube, on September 25, 1396.

Returning to the siege of Constantinople, he was again distracted by trouble in the East. The Anatolian rebels and dissidents proved easy enough to deal with; but beyond them lay another and greater enemy—Timur Lang, known to the West as Tamerlane. A man of humble origin, he had within a few years made himself master of the Mongol successor states in Central Asia. In 1380 he invaded Persia and in the next seven years overran the whole of it. He twice defeated the Mongol Khan of the Golden Horde in South Russia, raided India, and then overran Syria and exacted homage from the Mamluk Sultan. Timur was a Turk and a Muslim—but he was proud to relate himself to the Mongol Imperial house by marrying a princess of the line of Jenghiz Khan. Bayezid might claim the inheritance of the Seljuk Sultans of Rum—but Timur was heir of the Mongol Khans who had been their overlords. In 1394 he made his first attack in eastern Asia Minor, but was reluctant to press it against a Muslim sovereign engaged in Holy War on the borders of Islam. In the autumn of 1399 he reappeared—by now a mighty world-conqueror. Bayezid too had changed, and was no longer a chief of march-warriors but a rival Islamic monarch; the change was underlined by the dispossessed Anatolian emirs who took refuge at Timur's court. Even the might of the Ottomans was unable to resist the assault of the new conqueror from the steppe. On July 28, 1402, the two armies clashed in a plain near Ankara—and the Ottomans suffered a crushing defeat. Bayezid himself was taken captive, and he committed suicide eight months later; his Anatolian conquests reverted to the possession of the emirs whom he had ousted.

Bayezid's death was followed by ten years of crisis, rebellion, and civil war. The Ottoman dominions were reduced to those which he had inherited at his accession, and even those were disrupted by the ruinous struggle between his sons for the succession. In the course of these upheavals, the clash between Rumelia and Anatolia became clear—the former a new territory, peopled by march-warriors and colonists, the latter an old Islamic land. Prince Musa, who had shared his father's captivity and seen him die, rallied the support of the Rumelians, especially of the humbler people of the Balkans,

Christians as well as Muslims, peasants as well as frontiers-men, who feared and hated the growing power of the eastern lords and divines. Musa's regime was popular in its character and support—enough to frighten away the lords and dignitaries who had served him, and send them scuttling to join Prince Mehemmed in Anatolia. It was also Rumelian—and it is no accident that amid all the distractions of the struggle for the throne, he should have resumed the Holy War, recovered the Ottoman gains in Thrace, Thessaly, and Serbia, sent raiding parties as far as Carinthia, and, in 1410, laid siege to Constantinople.

Mehemmed was meanwhile rallying his forces in Anatolia, where he had succeeded in taking possession of all the Ottoman provinces. The social menace implicit in Musa's policies and actions enabled Mehemmed to win the support of the Balkan lords and princes—even of the prince of Serbia and the Emperor of Constantinople, who joined in this holy alliance against Musa. On July 5, 1413, in the mountains near Sofia, Musa was decisively defeated by his brother Mehemmed; after the battle he took refuge in flight, but was captured and strangled.

Two other brothers had already been eliminated, and with this victory, Mehemmed was at last in full possession of the Ottoman territories in Europe and Asia. His troubles were not yet over, however; in 1416 he had to face a dangerous revolt, probably social in origin, inspired and led by dervishes. It is significant that its spiritual leader was the famous Kadi Bedreddin, who had served as chief military judge in the army of Prince Musa. His teachings seem to have been a mixture of mysticism, religious communism, and a kind of interconfessionalism that sought to unite the different faiths.

Sultan Mehemmed I's reign was mainly concerned with restoring and consolidating the Ottoman state and realm, which he—and his successors—had for some years to protect from rebellions in various quarters and of various kinds. Under his son Murad II (1421–51), however, great and significant changes took place. The territorial expansion of the Empire was resumed, and the Ottoman forces won great and resounding victories against Greeks, Serbs, Hungarians, and Western Crusaders. In 1422, Murad laid siege to Constantinople, but the effort was premature, and he abandoned it. Instead, the Turks turned towards Europe. In 1430, Murad completed the conquest of Macedonia by seizing the seaport of Salonika, which the Greeks, in desperation, had sold to Venice three years previously. The further Turkish advance to the north encountered vigorous resistance from the Hungarians, and the siege of Belgrade in 1440 had to be abandoned. Further defeats by the Hungarians led Murad to agree to a ten-year peace, signed at Szeged in 1444, which, while it conceded some advantages to the Hungarians, safeguarded the Ottoman frontiers on the Danube.

Having thus, as he thought, secured the frontiers, Murad now abdicated in favor of his twelve-year-old son Mehemmed, and retired to the neighborhood of Bursa, in Asia Minor, to pursue a life of pious contemplation. As counselors to his son, he left the vizier Halil Pasha, scion of a family of high dignitaries who had served the Sultans for nearly a century, and Hosrev Molla, a prominent jurist and divine, probably of Christian extraction, who had just become Kadi of Edirne.

The temptation to break the truce was irresistible. In September of the same year, the Hungarians crossed the Danube and marched with their European allies southward into Bulgaria, and Murad, who had hastened back from Asia Minor, assembled his forces and hurried north to meet them. On November 10, 1444, at Varna, he inflicted a crushing defeat on the Hungarians, weakening the military power of the last state able to resist the Turks in Southeastern Europe, and dimming the dream of a European crusade to eject the Turks from the lands they had conquered.

Once again Murad attempted to retire, only to be recalled by the vizier Halil Pasha, to cope with a military mutiny in Edirne. The reluctant Sultan now remained on the throne, and during the last years of his reign undertook further campaigns in Greece, Albania, and Serbia. In 1448 a second battle at Kosovo gave the Turks a victory over an invading Hungarian army.

Important developments had also been taking place in Ottoman state and society. Since the time of Bayezid, the Ottoman Sultans had maintained a Muslim court on traditional lines, with courtiers and counselors and ministers of various kinds. Like the Muslim sovereigns of the East, they patronized poets, writers, and scholars; these last were sometimes able to render them great services. By now the Ottoman house needed a dynastic pedigree and tradition, and it is from this time that we can date the appearance, among the Ottomans, of what was to become the traditional historiography of the Imperial court. Accounts of the Oguz Turks, part legend, part fact, had been extant in various forms for some time. These were now studied and made the starting point of an

Ottoman historical tradition, in which the Ottoman ruling house was linked both with Turkish tribal legend and with the earlier Turkish Muslim Empires.

These new monarchical and dynastic ideas were sustained by the emergence of a class of trusted military and civil leaders, who were increasingly aware of and devoted to the principle of the Islamic dynastic state, and loyal to the house of Osman. They were immeasurably strengthened by the inauguration, some time earlier, of the *devshirme,* the levy of boys from among the Christian population of the Empire for recruitment into the Ottoman army and state service. By this means, the energies of the Christian population and the spirit of the march-warriors were both harnessed to the service of the Ottoman dynasty. At the same time, the lines of a solution were found to the increasingly urgent problem of associating, in harmonious collaboration, the two elements and traditions that made up the Ottoman Empire; the army, still dominated by the traditions of the border, and the state, deriving from the older patterns of the Islamic, Seljuk, and Mongol East.

In 1451, Murad achieved the final retirement of death, and was succeeded by his son Mehemmed II (1451–81), known as the Conqueror. Mehemmed inherited an empire that was still divided into two parts. Anatolia, even Ottoman Western Anatolia, was by now old Islamic territory, absorbed into and reshaped by the civilization of Middle Eastern Islam. Rumelia was newly conquered, still a frontier march, and was profoundly affected by the ideas and habits of the march-warriors who flocked there and by the eclectic and mystical faith of the dervishes who accompanied them. Between the two—between the old and the new capitals, Bursa of the theologians and Edirne of the march-warriors—a new link was needed. On May 29, 1453, two years after the Sultan's accession, the Janissaries made the final assault on the crumbling walls of Constantinople. The last Constantine was killed fighting among his troops; the crescent was raised above the dome of Santa Sophia; the Sultan of Rum took up residence in his Imperial city.

A Venetian visitor, Giacomo de' Languschi, or Langusto, met Mehemmed the Conqueror about the time of the Conquest. He describes him as

A young man of 26 [actually he was between 19 and 21], well complexioned, large in body rather than middling in height, noble in arms, of an aspect inspiring fear rather than reverence, sparing of laughter, a pursuer of knowledge, gifted with princely liberality, stubborn in purpose, bold in all things, as avid of fame as Alexander of Macedon. Every day he has Roman and other histories read to him . . . chronicles of the popes, the emperors, the kings of France, the Lombards; he speaks three languages, Turkish, Greek, and Slavonic. Diligently he seeks information on the position of Italy . . . the seat of the Pope, of the Emperor, and how many kingdoms there are in Europe, of which he has a map showing the states and provinces. Nothing gives him greater satisfaction and pleasure than to study the state of the world and the science of war. A shrewd explorer of affairs, he burns with the desire to rule. It is with such a man that we Christians have to deal. . . . He is vigilant, able to endure fatigue, cold, heat, thirst and hunger. . . . Now, he says, times have changed, so that he would go from the East to the West, as the Westerners had gone to the East.

The Empire of the world, he says, must be one, one faith and one kingdom. To make this unity there is no place in the world more worthy than Constantinople.

With the conquest of Constantinople, the last piece had fallen into place. The Sultan had sealed the union of the two continents, Asia and Europe, that formed his inheritance, and of the two traditions, Islam and the frontier, that had molded them. The principality of the march-warriors had become an empire; its chief was an emperor.

The remainder of Mehemmed's reign was occupied with an unceasing series of military campaigns, the main purpose of which was to consolidate and round off his empire. Many areas which had previously been under vassal or dependent rulers now came under direct Ottoman rule, thus preparing the way for new advances in the following century. In Europe, the Sultan subjugated the last Greek despotates in the Morea, made Serbia and Bosnia Ottoman provinces, and conquered a number of the Greek islands; in Asia he took Amasra from the Genoese, Sinope from its Muslim emir and Trebizond from its Greek emperor, and finally subjugated the Anatolian emirate of Karaman. Mehemmed, however, refused to be drawn further eastward; when challenged by Uzun Hasan, the ruler of the White Sheep Turcomans, he defeated him near Erzinjan in 1473, but made no attempt to follow up his victory, preferring instead to return to the West where his real interests lay. In a conversation quoted by the sixteenth-century historian Kemalpashazade, the Sultan explains his action. It was right and necessary, for reasons of state, to punish Uzun Hasan, with fire and sword, for his temerity;

it would have been wrong and unchivalrous to destroy his line, for "to seek the destruction of ancient dynasties of the great Sultans of the people of Islam is not a good practice." Besides, it would have distracted the Sultan from the serious business of the Holy War in Europe.

It was however in the East that the next great expansion was to take place, with far-reaching consequences. Mehemmed II himself is said to have been preparing an eastern campaign, of unknown destination, at the time of his death. Under his successor, Bayezid II (1481–1512), no major development occurred. Bayezid was a man of moderate and pious disposition. Among the Turks he was known as Veli—the saint—and he is famous as a builder of mosques and convents. In general his reign was a period of halt, during which the Ottomans rebuilt and developed their new capital and elaborated the structure of their new empire. In Europe, intermittent wars against the Poles, the Hungarians and their Venetian and Papal allies ended in 1503, with some Turkish territorial gains in the Morea and on the Adriatic. In addition, the Sultan granted to the Christian allies a seven-year truce; he was anxious to devote his attention to significant and dangerous developments in the East.

In the early years of the sixteenth century two changes took place which, in the long run, were to have the most far-reaching effects on the development of Ottoman state and society. The first was the rise to power, in Iran, of the Shi'ite dynasty of the Safavids; the second was the Ottoman conquest of the Arab lands.

Turkish Anatolia and, later, Rumelia had been the New World of the Islamic Empires, the colonial frontier to which they looked rather as Europe looked to the Americas. Even when the land of Rum became politically independent, it remained a colonial extension of the Turco-Persian culture which had its centers in Iran and Central Asia. In government and administration, in law and theology, in literature and the arts, the Seljuks and after them the Ottomans remained the pupils of the East and continued to rely very heavily on migrants from the East to staff and run their governments. The literature of Seljuk Anatolia was almost entirely in Persian, and when a literature in Turkish first appeared under the early Ottomans, it drew its inspiration from Persia and Central Asia. It is significant that when Murad II won his brilliant victory over the Crusaders at Varna in 1444 and captured a number of Frankish knights, it was across Persia to Herat that he paraded his resplendent captives, to display his success in the ancient centers whose applause he really valued.

The rise to power of a heretical dynasty in Iran, with its main focus in the northwestern area near the Ottoman borders, raised between the two countries the most impenetrable of all barriers—those of faith and of fear. There were millions of Sunni Muslims still in Persia; there were at least hundreds of thousands of Shi'ites of various persuasions in Anatolia, who could be suspected of favoring the heterodox Persian Shah. Both the Ottoman Sultan and the Safavid Shah were, for one another, heretics and usurpers, beyond the pale of toleration.

As early as 1502 Bayezid, already conscious of the danger to the Ottomans of the new Shi'ite emperor in Persia, had ordered the deportation of Shi'ite elements from Asia Minor to the Morea, and had mobilized on the Persian frontier. A Shi'ite revolt in central Anatolia, in 1511, underlined the danger. In 1512, faced with growing dangers, the aging Sultan was forced to abdicate and give way to his son Selim I (1512–20), to whom it fell to lead the Ottomans in the now inevitable war with Shah Ismail of Persia. On August 23, 1514, on the plain of Chaldiran, near the Turco-Persian border, the Ottoman Janissaries and artillery decisively defeated the armies of the Shah, and on September 7 the Sultan occupied the Persian capital of Tabriz. Despite their victories, however, the Ottomans were unable to maintain themselves on the plateau of Iran, and withdrew to Anatolia, leaving the Shah defeated and humbled, but still in control of his Shi'ite Empire of Iran. The fierce repression of Shi'ites in Turkey and of Sunnis in Persia watered their mutual hate and fear with the blood of martyrs.

Thereafter the Ottoman and Persian empires were divided by barriers hardly less important than those between the Ottomans and Western Christendom—and Iran herself lay as a barrier between the Ottomans and their Sunni brethren further to the east. Turkey was now cut off from Persia and Central Asia, which had contributed so much to her development in the past. She was now limited to her own spiritual and intellectual resources.

These were replenished from another and very different source, with the conquest, by the Ottomans, of the Arab lands. A swift campaign in 1516–17 destroyed the tottering Mamluk Sultanate and swept Syria and Egypt into the Ottoman Empire. With them the Ottomans also acquired some measure of control over western Arabia, including the Hijaz, with the two Holy Cities of Mecca and Medina. From Egypt, Ottoman suzerainty was extended southwards down both shores of the Red Sea, and westwards along the Barbary Coast to the borders of Morocco. In the East, the Ottomans succeeded in wresting Iraq from its Persian masters, and extending Ottoman power to the shore of the Persian Gulf.

With the exception of the Sultanate of Morocco, and of a few mountain and desert fastnesses where Arab independence still survived, the whole Arab world was now within the Ottoman Empire. The addition of so great a weight of territory and population with ancient traditions of their own could not fail to transform the very nature of Ottoman government.

There had, of course, been Arabic influence in Turkey before the conquest. Just as Persian had been the language of elegance and letters, so Arabic had been the language of theology and law, and a fair proportion of Ottoman men of religion either came from the Arab countries or had received their education there. But Ottoman civilization had derived from the East, not from the South—from the new and vital Perso-Turkish culture that had grown up in Seljuk and Mongol times, not from the declining silver age Arabic culture of the Mamluk Empire. The closing of the Eastern gate, and the simultaneous incorporation of the Arab lands in the Empire, opened the way to new influences from the Arab lands; Algerian corsairs, Egyptian spice merchants, Syrian divines, all found their way to the new imperial capital, to whose life all of them had a contribution to make.

The reign of Süleyman (1520–66)—called *Kanuni* by the Turks and the Magnificent by Europe—is rightly regarded as the apogee of Ottoman power and glory. The Sultan was well described by the Imperial ambassador, Ogier Ghiselin de Busbecq:

> If you Ask me, What manner of Man *Solyman* was? I'le tell you, He was an Ancient Man, his Countenance, and the Mean of his Body, was very Majestick, well becoming the Dignity which he bore; he was Frugal and Temperate, even from his Youth, tho' he might have taken a greater liberty to himself by the Rules of their own Religion. In his Younger Days he was not given to Wine, nor to Masculine Venery, which the *Turks* much delight in, so that his very Enemies could object nothing against him on those accounts; but that he was too Uxurious, and his over-Indulgence to his Wife made him give way to the Death of his Son *Mustapha,* yet that Crime was vulgarly imputed to that Ascendent she had over him, by reason of her Inchantments and Amatory Potions. This is certain, that after he once took her for his lawful Wife, he never had Carnal Knowledge of any other Women, tho' their laws did not forbid him. He is a very strict Observer of the Mahumetan Religion, and is as desirous to propagate *That,* as to enlarge the Bounds of his Empire.
>
> He is now Sixty Years of Age; and, for a Man of his Years, he enjoys a moderate proportion of Health, and yet his Countenance doth discover, that he carries about him some hidden Disease, 'tis thought a Gangrene or Ulcer, in the Thigh; yet at solemn Audiences of Embassadors, he hath a *Fucus* to paint his Cheeks, that he may appear sound and healthy to them, and thereupon be more dreaded by Foreign Princes, their Masters.

In Europe the Empire was extended by new victories. The seizure of Rhodes in 1522 established Ottoman sea power in the Eastern Mediterranean; the capture of Belgrade in 1521, and the great victory at the field of Mohács in 1526, opened the way to the conquest of Hungary and the bitter and sustained struggle with the Hapsburgs for Central Europe. In the south, Ottoman armies penetrated to southern Arabia and the Horn of Africa; in the east, Ottoman rule was established in Baghdad and, for a while, even in Tabriz. In the west, the corsair states of the Barbary Coast, now under the Sultan's suzerainty, carried Ottoman power into the Western Mediterranean and even—on raids—beyond the straits of Gibraltar. In 1529 an Ottoman army laid siege to Vienna; in 1537 an Ottoman expeditionary force tried to drive the Portuguese from the Indian Ocean; in 1553 the Sultan led an army into Persia; in 1555 an Ottoman fleet tried to take Malta. It was not realized until long afterwards that these were the high-water marks of the Ottoman tide.

The wide extent and military power of the Empire were paralleled in its thriving economy, its meticulous government, and its rich and brilliant culture. The capital city, already greatly developed under Süleyman's predecessors, became a vast and flourishing metropolis and a magnet to men of ambition and talent. From all over the Empire and beyond, poets and scholars, artists and architects, administrators and men of religion thronged to Istanbul, and helped to give its special and distinctive character to the new and vital Ottoman civilization that had grown from the merging of many traditions. It was in the days of Sultan Süleyman, and to no small extent under his patronage, that this civilization reached some of its greatest achievements. Baki the "Sultan of Poets," son of a muezzin in the Conqueror's mosque, wrote eulogies for the

living Süleyman, and an elegy on his death; Sinan, the greatest of Ottoman architects, embellished the city with splendid
mosques, finest among them the Süleymaniye, where the Sultan himself lies entombed; Ebu's-Suud, most distinguished of
the Ottoman doctors of the Holy Law, was chief mufti of the
capital, and an intimate friend of the Sultan. It was to him
that the aged Sultan, on his way to his final Hungarian campaign, wrote a moving personal letter, addressed to "my fellow in age and in sorrow, my brother in the world-to-come,
my comrade on the Right Road."

It was during the siege of Szigétvár, in Hungary, that, on
the night of September 5–6, 1566, the Sultan died in his tent.
The siege was still in progress; the heir to the throne was far
away. The Grand Vizier Sokollu Mehemmed Pasha therefore decided to keep the Sultan's death a secret. The Sultan's body was partially embalmed and carried in a litter for
three weeks until word was received that Selim II had been
safely enthroned in Istanbul. The secret was then revealed.
Süleyman's heart was buried in a mausoleum near Szigétvár; his body was taken to Istanbul and placed in the prepared tomb at the Süleymaniye mosque.

The dead Sultan behind the curtains of his litter with
armies still fighting under his command was a portent of the
fate of the Empire in the times that were to follow. For more
than a century after the death of Süleyman the Ottoman Empire remained a mighty power, and in 1683 was able to launch
its second great attack on Vienna. But the life had gone out
of it, and the succession of incompetents and degenerates who
followed the Magnificent on the throne of Osman symbolized
a deeper decay, that was nowhere better observed and under-

stood than in Istanbul itself. But the decline of Ottoman power was slow, fiercely resisted, and interrupted by several spurts of revival. In the twilight nostalgia of the seventeenth and eighteenth centuries, Ottoman culture was still to achieve some of its finest creations.

III. Sovereigns and Rulers

THE OTTOMAN SULTAN was a Muslim sovereign, and the only theoretical formulations that were made as to the source, nature, and limits of his power and jurisdiction were those of the Muslim jurists and scribes and their disciples. Ottoman theories of state and sovereignty have their roots in the constitutional provisions of the Holy Law of Islam; Ottoman writings on statecraft and government are a down-to-earth version of medieval Arabic and more especially Persian ethical and political treatises—their mirrors of magistrates and manuals for kings.

The Ottoman state began as a principality of march-warriors, and its head claimed no higher title than that of border chief (*uj begi*) or chief of the *gazis*—the fighters in the Holy War for Islam against the infidels. The early Ottoman rulers had been content with *gazi* titles; in an inscription of 1337, the second Ottoman ruler, Orhan, calls himself "Sultan, son of the Sultan of the *Gazis, Gazi,* son of *Gazi* . . . marchlord of the horizons, hero of the world." The fourteenth century poet Ahmedi, whose saga of the Ottomans is the earliest written Ottoman historical source, defines a *gazi* as "the instrument of the religion of God . . . a servant of God who cleanses the earth from the filth of polytheism . . . the sword of God." By their neighbors, the Ottoman rulers are described as princes—*beg* or *emir,* frequently as princes of the borders or the limits—*ujlar begi.* As the territory under the rule of the Ottomans grew in extent—particularly as they absorbed a large part of the old Islamic land of Anatolia, the Ottoman state began to undergo certain fundamental changes in its structure and purpose, becoming something less of a principality of frontiersmen and something more like a Muslim Empire of the classical kind.

The first of the Ottoman rulers to react in a clear and cogent manner to the challenge of these new developments was Bayezid the Thunderbolt, who, by adopting the title "Sultan of Rum," declared his claim to be the successor of the Seljuks and the sovereign of an Islamic Empire.

Bayezid's enterprise was premature. Within a few years his Anatolian conquests were lost and he himself, a prisoner in Timur's hands, took refuge from despair in suicide. But the interruption, terrible as it must have seemed at the time, was only temporary. Under his heirs and successors the process of expansion and transformation of the Ottoman state was continued.

Some fifty years after the conquest of Constantinople, the Turkish historian Tursun Beg wrote a history of the conqueror, which he presented to Mehemmed's son and successor Bayezid II. In the introduction to this biography Tursun

Beg sets forth some opinions on the necessity and nature of monarchy.

Man, he says, is by nature political and social; his way of life and his method of seeking a livelihood require him to live in groups. By the learned these are called civilized communities—that is to say, in common language, towns, villages, or nomadic tent families. Men need one another for mutual aid, and the desire to live in groups is therefore implanted in them. Since, however, they necessarily differ from one another in their innate aptitudes, habits, and desires, they tend to come into conflict. If they were left uncontrolled, these disputes and conflicts would ultimately defeat the purpose of mutual aid and indeed lead men to ruin and destroy one another. Therefore some form of organization is necessary to keep each man in his proper place and make sure that, content with his own rights, he does not try to infringe the rights of others. In this way effective mutual aid will be insured, and each, in his proper station, will carry out his proper task. This kind of organization is called polity, or political society. If it conforms to the basic principles of divine law and wisdom, and leads to a state of perfection in which men can realize the potentiality that has been put in them to achieve the two felicities (of this world and the next)—then it is what the philosophers call the divine polity, and they call the man who establishes it the Lawgiver. The men of religion call it *Sharī'a,* Holy Law, and the man who establishes it they call a Prophet.

If on the other hand the organization does not rise to that level, but simply appears to regulate human affairs at the discretion of the ruler—as for example in the case of the Mongol Jenghiz Khan—then it is called monarchical polity, or the discretionary rule of the sultan.

Whichever system it may be, its existence and endurance depend on there being a sovereign. There is no need for a prophet in every age, but there must always be a sovereign, for without a sovereign order would give way to anarchy.

The sovereign is therefore necessary, and the benefits he confers are shared by all. The gratitude, respect and obedience owed to him are further confirmed by the Koran and the Islamic traditions.

Having thus demonstrated that a sovereign is necessary and must be obeyed, Tursun Beg then goes on at some length to discuss the qualities that are needful in a sovereign, and to show how these are exemplified in the Ottoman Sultan. He enumerates four main virtues of rulers—justice, forbearance, moderation, and wisdom. Of these four, far and away the most important is justice. All mankind are in need of justice; even thieves and highwaymen have their own leaders who must share out justly, giving each his due—and if they did not their bands would not last a day. Justice means to maintain the proper order of the world, keeping each in his place and giving each his due, and preventing transgressions and infringements.

These reflections of Tursun Beg, with their echoes of Islamic jurisprudence, Greek philosophy, and Persian statecraft, are fairly typical of the prevailing system of political theory in the Ottoman Empire and indeed in other Islamic states, in the period between the destruction of the Caliphate and the impact of Western ideas. Like so much else in the composite culture of the Ottoman Empire, it reflects the coming together of many different trends and traditions.

By far the most important of these was the Islamic political tradition, in its various forms. Islam was born in a small town among a people just emerging from nomadism and still ruled by elected tribal chiefs—in effect by an oligarchy of prestige, birth, and wealth. Its earliest political memories are of an elected chief ruling by consent according to tribal custom. These memories are enshrined in the classical formulations of the early constitutional jurists of Islam; though rarely if ever put into effect, they have remained in the background of Islamic political ideas ever since.

In the strict theory of the Muslim jurists, there is no human legislative power. All law emanates from God, who is the sole source of both legislation and sovereignty. The Holy Law, promulgated by revelation and elaborated by authorized interpretation, is divine and immutable. The sovereign does not make law but is himself bound by the law, which is pre-existent to his office. The sovereign power is an expression of this law, maintained by it and maintaining it, to save the world from the ruin which would otherwise be caused by the natural destructiveness of man. Since the sovereign is the guardian of the divine law, obedience to him is a religious obligation; disobedience therefore is a sin as well as a crime.

In theory the sovereign is not really absolute. He is bound to uphold the Holy Law under which he holds office, and to which he is subject no less than the humblest of his slaves. He cannot abrogate or amend that law, since only God can make law and only the qualified interpreters of God's intention—i.e. the theologian-jurists of Islam—can interpret it. If the sovereign orders something contrary to the Holy Law, the duty of obedience lapses, for, as the Muslim jurists put it, "there is no obedience in sin" and "do not obey a creature against his Creator."

In fact, however, this restriction on the sovereign's absolutism was not very serious. For one thing, the law itself concedes him virtually absolute powers. For another, the law—and the jurists—never answered, or even posed, the question of how one tests the legality of a command by the sovereign, or deals with him if he acts against the law. Broadly speaking, the strength of what may be called public opinion obliged Muslim rulers to respect, at least outwardly, the basic beliefs and observances of the Muslim religion. But the custom of the people and the will of the ruler were in fact, and to some extent even in theory, accepted as sources of law, with their own agencies of enforcement.

Muslim political theory took new forms when Greek political ideas, notably those of Plato and Aristotle, became known to the Muslims. The ideas of Plato's *Republic* were modified and adapted to Islamic beliefs by the tenth-century Turkish philosopher Abu Nasr Al-Farabi (the Alpharabius of medieval Europe), whose work exercised a profound influence on subsequent writers. In Al-Farabi's Muslim version of the *Republic,* the sovereign power becomes more personal, more religious, and more autocratic. The republic becomes a "model city" bound together by a common faith, and the state merges into the person of a philosopher-king who, though still not hereditary, becomes a religious head and wields a vastly increased power reinforced by divine authority and sanction.

Even more potent than the influence of Greek philosophy was that of Persian wisdom and statecraft, which became known through Arabic translations and adaptations of earlier Persian writings, and through the personal impact of Persian ministers and rulers.

In a treatise presented by Kochu Bey in 1630 to Sultan Murad IV, the claim is made that since the days of the first caliphs no dynasty was ever so loyal and devoted to Islam, or showed so much respect to the doctors and doctrines of the Holy Law, as the Ottoman Sultans. The claim is by no means exaggerated. The deep religious earnestness of the Turkish dynasties, already noticeable under the Great Seljuks, continued and developed under the Ottomans. The Ottoman Sultans went further than any of their predecessors in making the Holy Law the effective law of the land; the behavior of the best of them shows a profound sense of mission and dedication—of duty to a sacred religious trust. True, the prevailing Islamic theories of government of their time show a movement from the Islamic ideal to the practical—but the conduct of state of the early Ottoman Sultans, when contrasted with that of their predecessors, shows a notable movement from the practical towards the Islamic ideal.

The Islamic tradition of politics and government came to the Ottomans in a late and developed form, modified by many influences and by long and painful experience. Perhaps for that very reason it was able to serve them as an effective guide to the conduct of state, with a set of rules of statecraft and government that were the practical obverse side of its theory of duties and obligations.

It was to this complex heritage of state, statecraft, and empire that the Ottomans succeeded when they grew from border chieftains into Muslim Sultans. But they were also Sultans, specifically, of Rum, and some have seen in Ottoman Istanbul a third, Muslim, Rome. Was "the Sultan in Byzance," as Milton called him, really the Emperor of a Turkish Rome—were his empire and his institutions of governments no more than the Byzantine Empire with new names and outward forms? The theory at one time commanded some support, but has not stood up to critical examination. The Byzantine Empire which the Ottoman encountered in the fourteenth and fifteenth centuries was no longer the Empire of Constantine, Justinian, or even Heraclius. It was a pale and feeble remnant of the past—and already half Westernized in its laws, its government, even in its institution of sovereignty. The final triumph of the Ottomans in 1453 laid the ghost of something that was already dead. Such inheritance as had remained had long since been claimed and carried off by the different heirs.

The Turks had had some share of this earlier inheritance. Something of Greece, Rome, and even Byzantium had become a part of classical Islam itself, and had come to the Turks as an unrecognized component of their Islamic heritage. In this respect it is significant that when the writer, Tursun Beg, quotes a version of Plato's *Republic* in about 1500, he derives his knowledge of it, not from Byzantine or Greek sources, but from medieval Persian and Arabic texts. The long coexistence of Greek and Turk in Anatolia at a time when the Byzantine Empire still retained some vigor, no doubt left its traces on the Seljuk state. These however were noticeable in everyday economic and social matters and local customs and practices; hardly at all in government and administration, where the Byzantine organization was destroyed and eliminated, and replaced by a classical Islamic governmental system, modeled on, and largely staffed from the sultanates in the East. It was from the Sultan of Rum, rather than any early or late emperor of Rome, that the Ottomans derived their theory and practice of government.

The most significant feature of the title Sultan of Rum is its connotation of a defined territorial sovereignty. The Great Seljuks had been Sultans of Islam—exercising the one and indivisible worldly power in the universal Muslim state. The Seljuks of Rum—and the Ottomans who revived their claims and titles—were Sultans of Rum, that is, of a definite country and people. The land of Rum was Anatolia, and for a time the Turks even called themselves Rum, after the country they inhabited. The extension of the Ottoman state into Europe reinforced this claim; the lands of Rum—of the Byzantine Empire or, rather, of Greek Orthodox Christendom—embraced territories in Europe as well as in Asia, and it was natural for the new masters of an important part of the estate to seek to acquire the whole of it. And so, to the old land of Rum—Anatolia—was added the new territory of Rumelia, both making up the patrimony of the Sultan of Rum.

In Ottoman writings of the fifteenth century the common title of their country is land of Rum, of their sovereign, Sultan of Rum. This marks him off from his Muslim neighbors, the sultans of Persia and Egypt, and expresses both the extent and the limits of his claims. The conquest of Constantinople was the completion, rather than the initiation, of a process of development.

Half a century later, the wars of Selim I against his Muslim neighbors, and the incorporation in the Ottoman Empire of the Arab lands in Asia and Africa, brought a reinforcement of the *Islamic* Imperial tradition.

The Empire was now no longer only that of Rum; it included the heartlands of Islam—the holy cities in Arabia, the seats of the great caliphs of Medina, Damascus, Baghdad, and Cairo. The Sultan of Egypt had gone; the heretical Shah of Persia was extruded from the comity of Sunni Islam—the Ottoman Sultan alone remained as the orthodox ruler of an Islamic state. True, there were still Sunni sovereigns in remote places like Morocco, Transoxania, and India, but these were too far away to make much impact. From North Africa right across the Middle East there was now but one Sunni Islamic Sultan—and he ruled over all the realms of the Caliphs, save only for such as had been lost to infidels or heretics.

In the preamble to the *ḳanuns* of Süleyman the Magnificent (1520–66), the Sultan describes himself as "Sultan of the Arabs and Persians and Rum." Süleyman is thus claiming sovereignty over the three major peoples of classical Islam. The title "Sultan of Rum" is replaced by *"Padishah-i Islam"* —the Emperor of Islam. In this title, which is commonly used by Ottoman historians and others to describe their sovereign, the wheel has come full circle; territorial sovereignty is lost again in a simpler and vaster claim that makes the Ottoman Sultan what he indeed was—the heir to the great universal Empires of Medieval Islam. The change was expressed in more than title: it can be seen most clearly in the growing interest in classical Muslim history and jurisprudence, in the elaboration of the orthodox Islamic apparatus of law, and in the rising influence of the Muslim jurists who were its accredited exponents.

Thus, in the course of two centuries, the institution of Ottoman sovereignty had passed through three major stages: those of the princes of the marches, the Sultan of Rum, the Padishah of Islam.

A major contribution of the steppe peoples to this stability was a stable principle of dynastic succession. The juristic doctrine of Islam was that the headship of the state was elective. In fact the elective principle remained purely theoretical, and Islam was ruled by a succession of dynasties, ranging from those of the caliphs themselves to the petty hereditary autonomies of the provincial governors. But the elective principle remained strong enough to prevent the establishment of any regular and accepted rule of succession.

The Turks introduced a new conception. Already in eighth-century Turkish inscriptions we find the notion clearly expressed of a family singled out by God to rule over the Turks and, more vaguely, other peoples and lands beyond them. The same idea reappears in an Islamic form in the correspondence of the Great Seljuks, with their claim to an inherited divine grant of kingship, and again, in a pagan form, in the chancery protocol of the Mongol Khans. For the Turks and Mongols, sovereignty was a family possession, and the whole family of the Khan or Sultan had a right to share in it. In the kingdom of the Seljuks we see the principle at work, whereby the brothers and cousins of the sovereign are admitted to a share of sovereignty. Under the Mongols, the whole vast Empire won by the conquests was divided up into family appanages, each of which was given to a son or grandson of Jenghiz Khan. We see it again among the Anatolian principalities, and perhaps also in the early Ottoman practice of appointing the sons of the Sultan to provincial governorships, in which they held miniature courts.

At the age of about fourteen, after their initiation to manhood by the rite of circumcision, the young princes were sent to govern provinces in Anatolia, where their aptitudes were observed and reported. In due course one of them was chosen as heir. To avoid the dangers of disputed successions, the Ottomans adopted what has come to be known as the "law of fratricide." This practice must have been an old one, since it is already referred to as an established rule (*nomos*) by the Byzantine Emperor John VI Cantacuzenus, who died in 1383. In the time of Mehemmed the Conqueror it acquired constitutional force, appearing in the fundamental laws of the Empire in these words:

> To whichever of my sons the Sultanate may be vouchsafed, it is proper for him to put his brothers to death, to preserve the order of the world. Most of the ulema allow this. Let them therefore act accordingly.

The principle underlying this law was an old and familiar one—that it was better for one or a few men to die, than that the world should be thrown into disorder. Accommodating theologians, with a little interpretative ingenuity, were able to find scriptural authority for this in a Koranic verse saying —in an entirely different context, of course—that discord is worse than killing. (Sura ii, 191, 217.)

For about a century and a half after the conquest of Constantinople, the rule of fratricide continued to be enforced by the Sultans. On the succession of each new Sultan, his surviving brothers were strangled with a silken bowstring, a form of execution reserved for the most exalted persons, whose blood it was impious to shed. European visitors to Turkey, familiar perhaps with royal murder but not with its legal enforcement, speak with horror of this law, which did, however, preserve the Ottoman Empire from the dynastic quarrels and wars that were causing so much trouble elsewhere.

In 1595, Sultan Mehemmed III, on succeeding to the throne, ordered the execution of his nineteen brothers, and also, it is said, of fifteen pregnant slave-women. It was the last such massacre. At the time of his death in 1603, he left only two sons, Ahmed and Mustafa, aged thirteen and twelve, both the sons of one mother. The fate of the dynasty depended on two untested boys, and it would have been too much of a risk to execute one of them. Ahmed became Sultan, but Mustafa was spared, and when Ahmed I died in 1617, with a boy of twelve as his eldest son, it was Mustafa who succeeded him. From this time onwards the rule was adopted that the succession went to the eldest surviving member of the house of Osman—a rule that worked well enough, though it did at times lay an unhealthy emphasis on survival. To Osman II (1618–22), the son of Ahmed I, belongs the distinction of having been the first Ottoman Sultan to be overthrown by a rising and killed. There were others after him.

With the law of fratricide, the princely apprenticeships as provincial governors also came to an end. Instead, the Ottoman princes spent their days in the *Kafes,* or cage, a group of buildings in the fourth court of the Imperial palace. There they went, with their mothers, their women and their slaves, to live a life of gilded imprisonment, from which they emerged only to die or to reign.

With such a system, it is not surprising that the Sultans who emerged to rule over the Empire during the seventeenth and eighteenth centuries were for the most part feeble in mind or body, sometimes dangerous degenerates. Only with the relaxation of the system, towards the end of the eighteenth century, did Sultans of real ability begin to appear again. In the meantime, there were others to take over the government of the city and Empire.

The first quality of kingship, says Tursun Beg, echoing the consensus of later Muslim political thought, is justice. "An hour's justice in judgment," says a tradition attributed to the Prophet, "is better than sixty years' worship." This is not an affirmation of the rights of the subject, whose position is sufficiently indicated by the parallel dictum that "sixty years of tyranny are better than an hour of civil strife." It does, however, reflect the accepted opinion on the basic obligation of government. Even the *Siyāset-nāme,* the famous Persian manual of statecraft written for the Great Seljuks, quotes an Arabic saying, repeated by many later writers, that "the world can go on with unbelief, but not with injustice."

But what is justice? For the classical jurists, justice meant the maintenance of the God-given law of Islam. Ghazali, writing in the age of the Seljuk Great Sultans, makes this the touchstone of righteous or unrighteous rule: "Justice may be known from tyranny by the Holy Law; let the religion of God and the law of the Prophet of God be the goal of every departure and the refuge of every return."

This Jewish and Pauline conception of justice as the maintenance of the divine and moral law was, however, overshadowed by another idea, of different origin. In the great majority of the ethical and political writers of the Eastern sultanates, the basic meaning of justice is balance, equipoise. Society is divided into classes, and each class has its proper place and function. The primary obligation of justice is to keep each class of society—and each individual within the class—in their proper stations, and thus to maintain the stability and order of the state. This idea, borrowed by Tursun Beg from the thirteenth century Persian Nasīr ad-Dīn Tūsī, goes back, in Islam, to the Islamized Republic of the tenth century philosopher Al-Farabi, and beyond him to its unconverted Platonic original. It was a doctrine well suited to the needs of an age when the loose and fluid social order of earlier times was giving way to a more rigid class system, in which the barriers of class and function were often reinforced by ethnic differences.

The Ottoman Sultans were always greatly—and consciously—concerned with maintaining the balance between the different elements on which their power rested; indeed, one of the favorite explanations given by those who examined the decline in Ottoman power and efficiency was the disturbance of that balance. But in the course of the centuries there were many changes in the composition of these dominant groups, and of their relation to one another.

There is a convergence of modern opinion that the interpretation of history as the struggle between economically defined classes for the control of the state, whatever relevance it may have to the West European history from which it was evolved, contributes little to the understanding of Oriental societies. Obviously there were economic classes in the Ottoman Empire, and there are not a few indications of struggle between them. The tenure and control of property, however, are weak and insecure as against the state; the economic classes are too vague and amorphous to play a significant role as such. Far more important than the ruling class—if indeed such a thing can be identified—was the ruling élite; the small, articulated, and interrelated groups of men who effectively controlled the day-to-day working of the apparatus of power, in association with the sovereign authority itself. There were several of these managerial or military élites, defined not primarily by economic class, but by skills, function, and method of recruitment. Their formation, rivalries, and vicissitudes are vital to the understanding of the history of the Turkish state.

The first Ottoman state was a principality of march-warriors, and the dominant group was that of the march-warriors themselves. Born and schooled on the frontier, their profession was war, their income booty, their religion the mystical, undogmatic creed of the dervishes who were their spiritual guides. There was however much to link the Ottoman *gazis* with their Christian opposite numbers—a common profession and way of life, common food, dress, and habits, and even, through the compulsory motherhood of raid and captivity, an occasional kinship of blood and language.

For several centuries now the military caste of Islam had been Turkish, and the Ottoman *gazis* had been overwhelmingly Turkish in origin and language—some of them adventurers and *condottieri* who had found their way to the western frontier, others Turkoman tribesmen migrating—or deported—under their own chiefs. But soon we find an important recruitment of local origin—Greek Christians who adopted Islam and threw in their lot with the Muslims. Some of these converts played a leading role among the *gazis;* of the four or five most ancient families of Ottoman nobility, two at least were of Greek ancestry.

As the Ottoman power spread into the Balkans, the Greeks were joined by many Slavs and Albanians who, for various reasons, decided to serve the Ottomans. Through victory and conquest, the *gazis* were now masters of vast lands in Europe, where a semi-Westernized Christian nobility had held privileges of a more or less Western feudal type. Among these *gazis* some settled down as military fief-holders with grants from the Sultans. It is from this time that we find a number of innovations, some of them possibly of West European origin, entering the Ottoman military and social system. The most important of these is the notion of a privileged military caste—the so-called *"askeris"*—enjoying a certain status by virtue of birth and descent.

The traditional Islamic society had, for all its political absolutism and quietism, been socially equalitarian. It had never developed anything like the caste system of the Hindu society to the east of it, or the aristocratic privilege of the Christian societies to the west.

In the early Ottoman Empire we find, for the first time in Islamic history, something like a real hereditary nobility—the *askeri* class. True, according to law, the *askeris* had no feudal or aristocratic privilege. They had no hereditary or prescriptive *right* to fief, office, or status, all of which could be conferred or withdrawn by the sultan at will. In fact, however, the sultan normally granted these fiefs or offices only to members of the *askeri* class, who were still considered as such even when not actually holding any fief or appointment. A clear distinction was maintained between the *askeris* and the subjects. The Muslim *askeris,* like the Muslim subjects, were bound by the provisions of the Muslim Holy Law, but were under the special jurisdiction of the *kadi-asker*—chief judge of the *askeris*—and not of the ordinary *kadis;* in administrative, fiscal, and disciplinary matters they were ruled by special codes of regulations issued by the sultan. These assured them important privileges and exemptions as against the subjects, who were forbidden to bear arms, ride horses, or hold fiefs.

That the term *askeri* denoted caste rather than function is made clear by the fact that it included retired or unemployed *askeris,* manumitted slaves of the sultan and of the *askeris,* the wives and children of *askeris* and also of the holders of religious offices at the sultan's court. The sultan could, by decree, demote an *askeri* to the subject class, or promote a subject to be an *askeri,* as a reward for exceptional services. Both were infrequent in the early period, and even such *askeris* as were demoted were still regarded as a separate category from the real "subjects." On the other hand it was regarded as contrary to the basic policies of the Empire to appoint subjects to *askeri* positions. The growth of this practice was regarded as an evil innovation and was adduced by Kochu Bey, writing in 1630, and by later Ottoman memorialists as one of the causes of Ottoman decline.

A significant feature of the early Ottoman system is that the distinction between *askeri* and subject is drawn neither on purely ethnic nor on purely religious lines. The non-military Muslim peasants and townsfolk of Asia were subjects no less than their Christian counterparts in Europe. On the other hand some of the Christian military gentry of the Balkans were enrolled in the Ottoman *askeri* class and granted fiefs by the sultan, at first without even the formality of conversion to Islam. In Ottoman Europe in the fifteenth century a certain proportion of the fief-holding feudal cavalry consisted of Christian gentry; by the sixteenth century almost all of them had been assimilated to Ottoman Islam.

The march-warriors had founded a state; the feudal gentry were building an empire—and their very success brought a new power into Ottoman society, that of the representatives of the classical civilization of Islam. Faced with the problems of governing and administering the territories and peoples over whom they ruled, the Ottoman sultans turned to the East for help and guidance, to the traditions—and the exponents—of the orthodox Islamic way of life. As the new territories were incorporated into the world of Islam, theologians and administrators from the East migrated to the Ottoman capital, bringing with them the skills, the methods, and the principles of the orthodox Islamic state. The early Ottoman chronicles, for the most part reflecting the outlook of the march-warriors, express very clearly their suspicion and resentment at the gradual imposition of political and religious orthodoxy. "When the ulema came to the Ottoman princes," says a popular anonymous chronicle of the fifteenth century, "they filled the world with all kinds of trickery. Before them nothing had been known of accounts or cadasters. When they arrived they organized accounts and cadastral surveys. They also introduced the practice of accumulating money and creating a treasury."

Government and law, taxation and registration, a treasury and a salaried staff—all these encroachments of the authority of the state were bitterly resented by the *gazis,* who clung tenaciously to the happy, carefree anarchy of the frontier. The consolidation of the Islamic state also brought them a new danger—that of religious orthodoxy. The religious faith of the marches had been simple and uncomplicated, with little concern for dogma or holy law. Heretics of all kinds had found a refuge, even a welcome, in the free lands of the frontier, and even the distinction between Muslim and unbeliever had been blurred in a way that was shocking to the exponents of Islamic orthodoxy. Muslim and Christian gentry served side by side in the Ottoman armies, and a vague, mystical, syncretistic faith found many points of contact between the two. The coming of the ulema and of the Holy Law laid down clear lines between orthodoxy and heresy, between Islam and unbelief—and aroused fierce opposition among the victims of its enforcement.

The Ottoman historiographical tradition assigns an almost demiurgic role to Kara Halil Hayr ed-Din Jandarli, the adviser of the second and third Ottoman rulers, and the founder of the Jandarli dynasty of viziers. The Jandarlis were members of the ulema class; they were also men of great and inherited wealth, with an understanding of commerce, politics and government. They, together with others of similar origin, began to coalesce into a class of administrators, counselors, and generals, who were aware of and devoted to the principle of the Muslim dynastic state, and loyal to the Ottoman reigning house.

One of the features of the classical Islamic state that was introduced to the Ottomans was the slave household. The nature and purpose of the system was well summed up by an English visitor to Turkey in the seventeenth century. After describing how youths of Christian parentage, "taken in War, or presented from remote parts," are trained and educated "for great offices of the Empire," he remarks:

> the Policy herein is very obvious, because the sons of Christians will hate their Parents being educated with other Principles and Customs; or coming from distant places have contracted no acquaintance, so that starting from their Schools into Government, they will find no Relations, or Dependencies on their Interests than that of their Great Master, to whom they are taught and necessity compels them to be faithful.

One of the problems of the autocratic ruler is to safeguard his autocratic power against the restraints imposed upon it or the dangers offered to it by an entrenched governing class. Even where there is no economically powerful class of property-holders, a military or bureaucratic élite may succeed in establishing itself in a position of effective—perhaps even hereditary—privilege. To prevent the formation of such élites or, if they existed, to keep them under effective control, was the objective of many despots in both East and West. To accomplish this, the despot needed a group of men without roots or loyalties outside his own service, owing their elevation not to rank or birth or status, but to his will alone, and bound to him by ties of both interest and loyalty.

In different societies the sovereign found different ways of recruiting and maintaining such a class of despotic agents. In ancient Persia, in China, at times in Rome and Byzantium, eunuchs formed a class of administrators and even soldiers who, precluded from family ambition, could serve the monarch against the old nobility without forming a new one themselves. In Europe, the Church provided the king with men of ability, learning, and ambition who, having made themselves as eunuchs for the love of God, could serve the king in the same capacity. Another method was to recruit men of humble or even alien origin into state office and, by constantly renewed recruitment, to prevent them from becoming a hereditary official caste. The famous Chinese examination system may, for a while, have been intended to serve this end. The most successful example of this technique is undoubtedly the Islamic slave army and slave state.

Political and military slaves are not unknown in the ancient empires, and seem to have had some importance in Persia in the Parthian period. The system of slave government, however, achieved its most developed and characteristic form in the Islamic state of the Middle Ages. The Muslim historians attribute the first creation of the slave army to the Abbasid Caliph Mu'tasim (reg. 833–842), the son of Harun al-Rashid. He, we are told, began to collect Turkish slaves from Central Asia while he was still a prince, and acquired a considerable number. After his accession to the caliphate he added many more and formed them into regiments of guards. This practice was followed by most of his successors.

In Asia Minor the slave system had been known in the Seljuk Sultanate and some of the older Turkish principalities of the center and the east. As one would expect, it did not exist among the free warriors of the marches. The introduction of this system to the Ottomans is one of the innovations attributed by the *gazi* historical tradition to the influence of theological interlopers from the East. According to the earliest chronicles, a theologian called Kara Rustem came from Karaman and pointed out to Jandarli Kara-Halil, then *ḳadi* of the army, that the sovereign's property was being lost. In accordance with the word of God one-fifth of the booty belonged to the sovereign, and this included the prisoners captured by the *gazis*. The Kadi informed Sultan Murad, who said that God's command must be obeyed. "This innovation," the chronicler remarks with obvious resentment, "was the work of a pair of theologians." One out of every five of the captives was taken for the Sultan.

> Many young men were collected and brought to the Sultan. Halil said: "Let us give them to the Turkomans and let them learn Turkish. Then we shall make soldiers of them." And so it was done. There were more of them every day and they all became Muslims. The Turkomans made use of them for some years, and then brought them to the Gate. They gave them white caps to wear . . . and called them by the name of *Yeni Cheri*—new soldiers.

Thus was born the famous corps whom Europe knew as the Janissaries.

In the name of God, the Sultan's Islamic advisers had brought law and taxation—the royal fifth and the royal slave establishment. By this time the Turks were no longer the slaves but the enslavers. The Turks of Anatolia were already an old Muslim people, protected by both law and long tradition from enslavement. But an effective substitute was ready to hand. Just as centuries before the Muslim march-warriors in the Central Asian borders of Islam had captured and enslaved the heathen Turks, so now the Muslim Turkish *gazis* on the western borders made war against their Christian adversaries and treated their captives, in accordance with the laws of Islam, as booty. Like the Muslim caliphs and emirs of Baghdad and Persia, the Ottoman sultans too formed their foreign legion of slaves—this time from among their Christian prisoners.

Recruitment from prisoners, however, was sporadic and unsatisfactory. The intakes were irregular, and the full-grown soldiers that they provided must have been far less easily assimilated than the barbarian youths who had formed the recruits of the early Mamluk armies. Sometime in the late fourteenth century the Ottomans applied a new method—the famous *devshirme,* or levy of boys, collected from the Christian village population for recruitment into the Ottoman army and state service. This system, of doubtful propriety in Muslim law, nevertheless became a regular Ottoman institution, and remained in operation until the seventeenth century, and possibly longer.

By this device a double purpose was served. On the one

hand a plentiful supply of slaves was assured, to meet the needs of the Sultan's army and household. On the other, the energies of Rumelia were harnessed to the Ottoman state. Every five years special commissioners traveled through Rumelia—later also Anatolia—and made a selection of boys for the *devshirme*. These were then converted to Islam and taught Turkish—often by being placed as retainers, or esquires, with members of the feudal cavalry or *sipahi* class. At an early stage they were sent to an assembly point where they were assigned by an interviewing board to different branches of the sultan's service. The majority became military cadets, and eventually graduated into the corps of Janissaries or another branch of the paid, standing army. The cream of the intake were assigned to the palace school of pages, where after a long and elaborate education they became members of the imperial household and eligible for the highest government appointments, most of which, even the grand vizierate, were normally filled from this source. It was in this way, and in this way alone, that, until the sixteenth century, the Janissary corps were recruited. No freeborn Muslim could enter, and even the children of the members were ruthlessly excluded.

Through the *devshirme,* supplemented with slaves acquired by purchase or as tribute, the sultans were able to muster a vast body of trained soldiers and administrators, with no loyalties other than to the corps and the household—and at the same time to prevent the formation of a hereditary caste of rulers. The military slave establishments were known as *Kapi Kulu*—Slaves of the Gate—to indicate their relationship to the sultan, and to mark them off from the freeborn feudal levies. Their bondage, it may be noted in passing, was more political than legal. Though formerly slaves, they exercised the rights of free men in matters of property, marriage, and personal status, and were not treated as slaves in the juridical sense; they were however deemed the property of the sultan, and they, their lives, and their possessions were wholly at his disposal.

Between the Slaves of the Gate and the feudal gentry there was an obvious clash of interests, in which the former were for long victorious. The two had not always been distinct and separate. In the early period many of the *sipahis* had themselves employed slave retainers, and many members of the slave establishment had made their way into the feudal gentry. Both enjoyed the status of *askeri,* and in time the form of fief-holding was modified so as to strengthen the sultan's hold even over the feudal cavalry. By the late fifteenth century the old aristocratic and feudal families were losing their influence, and the slaves were dominant in both central and provincial government. This process was accelerated by the growing use of firearms, which increased the importance of the standing, professional slave regiments and reduced that of the feudal cavalry levies. By the reign of Süleyman the Magnificent, when the classical Ottoman system was at its peak, all the different elements of the Ottoman ruling class were integrated into a single centralized ruling institution, under the absolute control of the sovereign.

In November, 1553, the English traveller Anthony Jenkinson, then in Syria, saw the Sultan Süleyman the Magnificent and his army in all their glory, on their way to the wars in Persia. He describes their entry into Aleppo:

There marched before the Grand *Signior,* otherwise called the Great Turke, 6,000. Esperes [*Sipahis*], otherwise called light horsemen, very braue, clothed all in scarlet.

After marched 10,000. men, called *Nortans* [*?Orta*], which be tributaries to ye Great Turk, clothed all in yellow veluet, and hats of the same, of the Tartarie fashion, two foote long, with a great robe of the same colour about their foreheads, richly decked, with their bowes in their hands, of the Turkish fashion.

After them marched foure Captaines, men of armes, called in Turkish *Saniaques* [*Sanjak*], clothed all foure in crimson veluet, euery one hauing vnder his banner twelue thousand men of armes, well armed with their morrions [helmets] vpon their heads, marching in good order, with a short weapon by their sides, called in their language *Simittero.*

After came 16,000. Ianizaries, called the slaues of the Grand *Signior,* all afoote, euery one hauing his harquebushe, who be his gard, al clothed in violet silke, and apparelled vpon their heads with a strange forme, called *Cuocullucia,* fashioned in this sort: the entring in of the forehead is like a skull made of white veluet, & hath a traine hanging downe behinde, in manner of a French hoode, of the same colour, and vpon the forepart of the saide skull, iust in the middes of his forehead, there is standing bolt vpright like a trunke of a foote long of siluer, garnished most richly with Goldsmiths worke, and pretious stones, and in the toppe of the saide trunke a great bush of feathers, which wauereth vp and downe most brauely when he marcheth.

After this there came 1,000. pages of honour, all clothed in cloth of golde, the halfe of them carying harquebushes, and the other halfe Turkish bowes, with their trusses of arrowes, marching in good order.

Then came three men of armes well armed, and vpon their harnesse coates of the Turkes fashion, of Libard skinnes, and murrions vpon their heads, their speares charged, and at the ende of their staffe, hard by the head of ye speare, a horse taile died in a bloody colour, which is their ensigne: they be the challengers for the Turkes own person.

After them came seuen pages of honour in cloth of siluer, vpon seuen white horses, which horses were couered with cloth of siluer, all embrodered and garnished with pretious stones, emerauds, diamonds, and rubies most richly.

After them also came six more pages of honour, clothed in cloth of golde, euery one hauing his bowe in his hand, and his fawchine of the Turks fashion by his side.

Immediately after them came the Great Turke himselfe, with great pompe & magnificence, vsing in his countenance and gesture a wonderfull maiestie, hauing onely on each side of his person one page clothed with cloth of golde: he himselfe was mounted vpon a goodly white horse, adorned with a robe of cloth of golde, embrodered moste richly with the most pretious stones, and vpon his head a goodly white tuck, containing in length by estimation fifteene yards, which was of silke and linnen wouen together, resembling something Callicut cloth, but is much more fine and rich, and in the toppe of his crowne a little pinnach of white Ostrich feathers, and his horse most richly apparelled in all points correspondent to the same.

After him followed six goodly young Ladies, mounted vpon fine white hackneis, clothed in cloth of siluer, which were of the fashion of mens garments, embrodered very richly with pearle, and pretious stones, and had vpon their heades caps of Goldsmiths worke, hauing great flackets of heare hanging out on each side, died as red as blood, and the nailes of their fingers died of the same colour, euery of them hauing two eunuches on each side, and little bowes in their hands, after an Antike fashion.

After marched the Great Basha, cheefe conductor of the whole armie, clothed with a robe of Dollymant crimson, and vpon the same another short garment very rich, and about him fiftie Janizaries afoote, of his owne gard, all clothed in crimson veluet, being armed as the Great Turks owne Janizaries.

Then after ensued three other Bashas, with slaues about them, being afoote, to the number of three thousand men.

After came a companie of horsemen very braue, and in all points well armed, to the number of foure thousand.

All this aforesaid armie, most pompous to behold, which was in number foure score and eight thousand men, encamped about the citie of *Aleppo,* and the Grand *Signior* himselfe was lodged within the towne, in a goodly castle situated vpon a high mountaine: at the foote whereof runneth a goodly riuer, which is a branch of that famous riuer *Euphrates.*

The rest of his armie passed ouer the mountaines of *Armenia,* called nowe the mountaines of Camarye, which are foure daies iourney from *Aleppo,* appointed there to tarie the comming of the Grand *Signior,* with the rest of his armie, intending to march into Persia, to give battell to the Great Sophie. So the whole armie of the Grand *Signior,* containing as well those that went by the mountaines, as also those that came to Aleppo in companie with him, with horsemen and footemen, and the conductors of the camels and victuals, were the number of 300,000. men.

The camels which carried munition and victuals for the said armie, were in number 200,000.

IV. Palace and Government

THREE WEEKS after the fall of Constantinople, Sultan Me-hemmed the Conqueror left his new capital for Edirne, where he spent some months in the new palace he had built there. A year later he returned to Constantinople, and established his residence in a palace on the third hill, in the center of the city, on the site later occupied by the Ottoman Ministry of War, and at present by the University of Istanbul. About a dozen years after the conquest, the Sultan decided to build a new palace, in a more secluded position, and with ample space for the growing and variegated imperial household. He chose the promontory that juts into the sea between the Golden Horn and the Sea of Marmara, the site of a Byzantine acropolis; it has been known ever since as Sarayburnu—Se-raglio Point.

The word *Saray* is of Persian origin, and means a residence or palace. In Ottoman usage it denotes the whole complex structure of the imperial palace, court, and household. The

European derivatives of the word—Seraglio, Serail—are often restricted to that part of the imperial household which most attracted the attention of European visitors—the women's quarters. Turkish usage knows no such limitations, and applies the term *Saray* to the whole and not just part of the palace.

The construction of the palace was begun in about 1465 and completed in 1478. It was called the New Palace, in contrast to the Old Palace on the hill; it is, however, more commonly called by the name of the old fortified sea gate at the Point—Topkapi, the Cannon Gate. The Topkapi Palace remained the residence of the Ottoman sultans and court until the nineteenth century, when they moved to new buildings elsewhere. It was at that time that the confusing practice arose of calling the Topkapi or New Palace the Old Palace, in contrast to the still newer buildings to which the Sultan had gone. A series of great fires—notably those of 1574, 1665, and 1862—destroyed the greater part of the original buildings, which were replaced by new ones; the basic plan and division, however, seem to have undergone little change.

The Ottoman Saray was from the first a subject of fascinated attention from Europeans, and many descriptions, of varying accuracy and authenticity, were written for the instruction of the curious. Very few of them seem to be based on firsthand knowledge. One of these was written by Domenico Gerosolomitano, a Rabbi from Jerusalem, later a convert to Christianity, who served as physician to Murad III. His account, still unpublished, may underlie many of the descriptions by seventeenth-century European writers. One of the earliest and best of these is Ottaviano Bon, envoy of the

Republic of Venice in Istanbul from 1606 to 1609. His *Description of the Grand Signior's Serraglio* was adapted into English by his contemporary Robert Withers, who spent some time in the house of the English ambassador in Istanbul. The *Description* opens with an account of the Seraglio precincts:

The Serraglio, wherein the Grand Signior dwelleth, with all his Court, is . . . inclosed with a very high and strong wall, upon which there are divers watch-towers, and is, by computation, about three Italian miles in compasse. It hath many Gates . . . but the chiefest Gate (which indeed is a very stately one) is one of those towards the Citie; and by it everyone goeth in and out daily; the others being kept shut, till such times as the King, or some of the principall Officers of the Serraglio shall cause any of them to bee opened. . . .

The aforesaid chiefe and common Gate is in the day time guarded by a great companie of Capoochees [*Kapiji*], which change their watch by turnes, and in the night likewise by others; all which Capoochees are under the command of a Capoochee Bashee [*Kapiji-bashi*]. . . . And without the Gate, about ten or twelve paces off, there stands a little House made of boords, upon wheeles, in which every night a Companie of Janizaries doe watch, who upon any occasion are ready to awake those within, and to give them notice of whatsoever sudden accident may happen without. . . .

In this Serraglio there are many stately Roomes, appropriated to the seasons of the yeere. . . .

There is amongst the aforesaid Roomes the Chamber into which the Grand Signior repaireth, when he is to give audience to Ambassadors, to the Bashawes on the dayes of publique Divan, and to those who being to depart upon any weighty service, or employment, are to take their leave of him; as also to such who, after the limited time of their government abroad is expired, do return to Constantinople, to give account to his Majesty of their carriage in their several places. . . .

There are two large buildings; one of which is the Hazineh or private Treasurie, and the other the King's Wardrobe. These are two very handsome buildings, and secure, by reason of the thicknesse of their walls, and strong Iron windowes, and have each of them an Iron doore, both which are alwaies kept shut, and that of the Hazineh sealed with the King's seale. . . .

At the first entrance into the Serraglio, there is a very large and stately Gate, in the Porch whereof, there is alwaies a Guard of about fiftie men with their weapons by them; as Peeces, Bowes and Swords: and having passed this Gate (through the which the Bashawes and other Great men may ride on horse-backe) there is a very Spacious Court-yard about a quarter of an Italian mile in length, and almost as much in bredth; and on the left hand of the Court neere unto the gate there is a place to shelter the people and horses in raynie weather: and on the right hand there is an Hospital, for such as fal sick in the Serraglio. . . . it is kept by an Eunuch, who hath many servants under him to attend upon the diseased. . . .

Having passed through the aforesaid Court, there is a second gate (at which the Bashawes alight) somewhat lesse than the former, but more faire and costly; under which there is also a stately Porch, where there is likewise a guard of Capoochees. . . . then there is another Court lesse than the former, but farre more beautifull, by reason of the delicate Fountaynes, and walkes enclosed with Cypresse Trees, and the fine greene grasse-plots in which the Gazells doe feed, and bring forth young . . . in this court (the Grand Signior only excepted) every one must goe on foot: On both sides of the said Gate, there is an open gallerie underset with very stately Pillars, without the which the Chiaushes [*Chaush*], the Janizaries, and the Spahees [*Sipahi*], doe use to stand all along in rankes very wel apparelled, at such times as there is a great Divan held for the comming of any Ambassador, to kiss the Grand Signior's hand.

In the said Court on the right hand are all the Kitchins, being in number nine, all which have their Larders, and severall Officers for their service. . . .

And on the left side of the Court there is the King's Stable of about thirtie, or thirtie five very brave Horses, which his Highnesse keepeth for his exercise, when he pleaseth to runne, or sport with his Gentlemen the Aghaes in the Serraglio. . . .

Neere adjoyning to the said Stable, are certayne buildings for the service of the Officers of the Divan; and having passed two thirds of the Court, there is the Roome wherein the Divan is kept; unto which joyneth the Hazineh (treasury), called the outward Hazineh, the which the Divan being ended, is sealed with the chiefe Viziers Seale: And even with the room where the Divan is kept but somewhat behind it towards the left hand, is the Gate which leadeth into the womens Lodgings, called the Queenes gate, which is kept and guarded by a company of blacke Eunuches.

The aforesaid second Court endeth at a third Gate, called the Kings Gate, which leadeth into the Roomes and Lodgings kept apart for himself, and such Gentlemen as attend upon him continually; neither may any one enter therein, but by absolute leave from the Grand Signior (speaking of men of great qualitie) but such as are belonging to the Butterie or Kitchin, and Physicians, Caters and Sewers, may goe in and out with leave only of the Capi Agha [*Kapi Aga*], who is the

Chiefe Chamberlaine of the Serraglio, and to him is committed the keeping of that Gate; and he is alwayes at hand (by reason his Lodging is neere) with a Company of white Eunuches about him like himselfe. So that, what is reported of things within this Gate is for the most part by relation; for, either one may not see them, or if hee doe see them, it must bee when the King is absent. . . .

Having passed the third Gate (the which hath also a very faire Porch) immediately is seene the aforesaid Roome appointed for publique audience. . . .

The Roome which is called the publike Divan, hath been built of late yeeres. It is foure square, and about eight or nine paces every way from side to side; it hath behind it another Roome for the service thereof, and one also at the coming in to the Divan, on the right hand, divided only by a woodden rayle: with many other Roomes somewhat distant from it, which serve for the expedition of sundry businesses: This Divan is called publike, because any kinde of person whatsoever (as well stranger as native), publiquely and indifferently, may have free accesse unto it, to require justice, to procure grants, and to end their Causes and Controversies, of what nature, condition, or import so ever they bee.

The three successive gates described by Bon, leading into the inner quarters of the palace, are the Imperial Gate, the Middle Gate, and the Gate of Felicity. The area between the first and third gates was known as the *Birun,* the Outside, and was occupied by the so-called Outside Services of the Imperial Household. These fall into six main groups.

The first of these consisted of men who belonged, by education and status, to the ulema, the professional men of religion. They comprised the preceptor of the sultan, a religious functionary of high dignity and reverence; the palace chaplains; the chief astrologer, and—since medical education was also a preserve of the ulema—the chief physician, chief surgeon, and chief oculist of the household. The chief physician was senior to his two colleagues, and presided over a corps of palace physicians, including a number of Jewish doctors as well as Muslim ulema.

A second group were the four special commissioners *(emin)* each with his own staff, in charge of a department of the imperial household. The city commissioner *(shehr-emini)* was responsible for the construction, care and maintenance of buildings in the capital belonging to the royal domain, and also served as a kind of intendant of the palaces, concerned with the pay and expenses of the household, and the provision of food, clothing and other needs for its consumption. His staff included the chief architect, the water inspector, the stores commissioner, and other functionaries concerned with different branches of supply and maintenance.

Another *emin* whose functions made him a public as much as a palace official was the commissioner of the mint *(darphane emini)*, which in the seventeenth century was transferred to a building in the palace grounds, near the Imperial Gate. The two remaining commissioners were concerned with the palace kitchens, and with the supply of fodder to the palace stables.

The largest and most important group of officers in the Outside Service were the agas of the imperial stirrup *(agayan-i rikâb-i hümayun)*. The stirrup had been an emblem of sovereignty among the Turks since Seljuk times; the agas of the stirrup owed their title to their attachment to the imperial household, and to the privilege some of them had of holding the stirrups and bridle when the sultan mounted his horse. Their numbers and status changed in different periods; as with the commissioners, several of them had duties extending far beyond the imperial household. As listed in the *Kannunname* of Mehemmed the Conqueror, they include the aga of the janissaries, the agas of the six regiments of household cavalry, and the agas of the gunners and armorers. Other agas of the stirrup, directly concerned with palace matters, were the standard-bearer (*mir-i alem*), the chief and deputy chief of the gate-wardens (*ḳapiji*), the master of the stables (*mir-ahor*), the chief pursuivant (*chaush-bashi*), the chief taster (*chashnigir-bashi*), and the chief falconer (*chaḳirji-bashi*).

Two other corps, not forming part of the agas of the stirrup, were the *müteferriḳas* and the *baltajis*. The former were a kind of élite guard, recruited from the sons of high dignitaries, and joining the sultan's personal escort. Splendidly mounted and accoutered, they each had their own slave retainers, and were often seconded on important missions. The *baltajis,* literally axemen, were originally a kind of army pioneer corps; after the conquest of Constantinople, they became a palace guard, stationed partly at the Old and partly at the New Saray. The *baltajis* of the Topkapi Palace formed a privileged corps. Their duties were chiefly concerned with the protection of the harem, and to prevent them from casting unauthorized glances within the forbidden precincts, they wore special caps with long flaps on each side, made of cloth or gold lace, in appearances like lovelocks. Because of this they were known as the *zülüflü baltajis*—the lock-wearing or blinkered axemen. Until the eighteenth century, they were under the command of the chief white eunuch.

The remainder of the Outside Service was made up of a variety of smaller specialized corps and crafts. Among the former were archers and ceremonial guards and escorts, pursuivants, messengers and runners, bandsmen and flag-bearers; among the latter are the cooks and bakers, tailors and cobblers, launderers and cleaners, and the innumerable other artisans and specialists whose services were needed at the palace.

The first court, between the Imperial and Middle gates, held a variety of buildings—guardrooms and dormitories, depositories and depots, and, at a later date, the mint. It was open to the public, and was generally crowded with people. The second court, between the Middle Gate and the Gate of Felicity, was open only to those with business at the palace. A rectangle of about 150 by 120 yards, it served as a parade-ground on ceremonial occasions. Its most important buildings were the Treasury and the *Divanhane,* where the Imperial Council met, and where the sultan received the ambassadors of foreign states.

The ceremonies followed on those diplomatic occasions have often been described. The reception of Edward Barton, the second English envoy in Istanbul, may serve as an example:

> Our Ambassador likewise apparelled in a sute of cloth of silver, with an upper gowne of clothe of gold, accompanied with 7 gentlemen in costly sutes of Sattin, with 40 other of his men . . . at his house tooke boate: at whose landing the shipp discharged all her ordinance, where likewise attended 2 Bassas

with 40 or 50 Chauses to accompany ye ambassador to the court, and also horses for the ambassadour & his gentlemen, very richly furnished with Turkish servants, attendat to take the horses whe they should light. The ambassador thus honourably accompanied, the Chauses foremost, next his men on foote all going by two and two himselfe last with his Chause and Drugaman or Interpreter and 4 Janisaries, which he doeth usually entertaine in his house to accompany him continually abroad, came to the Seraglio about an English mile from the water side, where first hee passed a great gate into a large court (much like the space before Whitehall gate) where he with his gentlemen alighted and left their horses. From hence they passed into another stately court . . . where all the court was with great pompe set in order to entertaine our ambassador. Upon the right hand, all the length of the court was a gallerie arched over, and borne up with stone pillars, much like the Roiall Exchange, where stood most of his guard in rankes from the one end to the other in costly array, with round head pieces on their heads of metall and gilt over, with a great plume of fethers somewhat like a long brush standing up before. On the left hand stood the Cappagies or porters and the Chauses. All these courtiers being about the number of 2000 (at I might well gesse), most of them apparelled in clothe of gold, silver, velvet, sattin and scarlet, did together with bowing their bodies, laying their heads upon their brests in courteous maner of salutation, entertain the Ambassador who likewise passing between them & turning himselfe sometime to the right hand and sometime to the left answered them with the like. As he thus passed along, certaine Chauses conducted him to the Douan, which is the seat of Justice . . . which place is upon the left side of this great court, whither the ambassador with his gentlemen came, where hee found the Vizir . . . who with great shew of kindness received him; and after receit of her maiesties letters and conference had of the Present, of her Maiesties health, of the state of England, and such other matters as concerned our peaceable traffique in those partes: dinner being prepared was by many of ye courtiers brought into another inner roome next adjoining, which consisted of an hundred dishes or ther abouts, most boiled & roasted, where the ambassadors accompanied w^t the Vizirs went to dinner, his gentlemen likewise with the rest of his men having a dinner with the like varieties prepared upon ye same side of the court, by themselves sate downe to their meat, 40 or 50 Chauses standing at the upper end attending upon the gentlemen to see them served in good order; their drinke was water mingled with rosewater & sugar brought in a Luthro (that is a goate's skinne) which a man carrieth at his backe, and under his arme letteth it run out at a spout into cups as men wil call for it. The dinner thus with good order brought in and for halfe an houre with great sobrietie and silence performed, was not so orderly taken up; for certaine Moglans [*ajemioglans*] officers of the Kitchen (like her Maiesties blacke guard) came in disorderly maner and tooke away the dishes, and he whose hungry eie one dish could not satisfie, turned two or three one into the other, and thus of a sudden was a cleane riddance made of all.

The Divan Chamber was as far as the foreign visitor—apart from ambassadors received in audience—was allowed to penetrate. Beyond the Gate of Felicity lay the *Enderun,* the inner apartments, one section of which was the *Harem-i Hümayun,* the Imperial Gynaeceum. One of the few foreigners who claim, with reasonable plausibility, to have entered the inner apartments was Thomas Dallam, an English organ maker who went to Istanbul in 1599 to present an organ which he had made as a gift from Queen Elizabeth to the Sultan.

The 12, [October] beinge Fridaye, I was sente for to the Courte, and also the Sondaye and Monday folloinge, to no other end but to show me the Grand Sinyors privie Chamberes, his gould and silver, his chairs of estate; and he that showed me them would have me to sitt downe in one of them, and than to draw that sord out of the sheathe with the which the Grand Sinyor doth croune his kinge.

When he has showed me many other things which I wondered at, than crossinge throughe a litle squar courte paved with marble, he poynted me to goo to a grait in a wale, but made me a sine that he myghte not goo thether him selfe. When I came to the grait the wale was verrie thicke, and graited on bothe sides with iron verrie strongly; but through that graite I did se thirtie of the Grand Sinyor's Concobines that weare playinge with a bale in another courte. At the firste sighte of them I thoughte they had bene yonge men, but when I saw the hare of their heades hange doone on their backs, platted together with a tasle of smale pearle hanginge in the lower end of it, and by other plaine tokens, I did know them to be women, and verrie prettie ones in deede.

Theie wore upon theire heades nothing bute a little capp of clothe of goulde, which did but cover the crowne of her heade; no bandes a boute their neckes, nor anythinge but faire cheans of pearle and a juell hanginge on their breste, and juels in their ears; their coats weare like a souldier's mandilyon, some of reed sattan and som of blew, and som of other collors, and grded like a lace of contraire collor; they wore britchis of scamatie, a fine clothe made of coton woll, as whyte as snow and as fine as lane; for I could desarne the skin of their thies throughe it. These britchis cam doone to their mydlege; som of them did weare fine cordevan buskins, and som had their leges naked, with a goulde ringe on the smale of her legg; on her foute a velvett panttoble 4 or 5 inches hie. I stood so long loukinge upon them that he which had showed me all this kindnes began to be verrie angrie with me. He made a wrye mouthe, and stamped with his foute to make me give over looking; the which I was verrie loth to dow, for that sighte did please me wondrous well.

Beyond the Gate of Felicity were the third and fourth courts, with a number of side-courts and groups of buildings. Until the end of the sixteenth century the Inside Services were controlled by the eunuchs, of whom there were two corps, the black eunuchs and the white eunuchs, each with their own ladder of seniority and promotion. The chief of the black eunuchs was the *Kizlar Agasi,* the aga of the girls; the chief of the white eunuchs was the *Kapi Agasi,* the aga of the gate, i.e. of the Gate of Felicity. At first the white eunuchs were predominant, but from the end of the sixteenth century they lost ground, and suffered a diminution of both numbers and status. In the harem, control passed to the black eunuchs; in the other departments of the Inside Service, to the so-called pages who made up the bulk of its personnel.

These were boys of Christian origin, recruited into the Ottoman service by the *devshirme,* and called *ajemi-oglans* —foreign boys, probably with the meaning of novices or raw recruits. Those selected for the palace service were known as *ich-oghlans*—inside boys, and on becoming full members of the household as agas of the inside. After a period of training and general education at one of the palace schools, they were appointed to the Inside Service.

There were six major divisions, known as chambers. They were, in ascending order of promotion, the Greater and Lesser chambers, where the cadets received further instruction; the Falconer's Chamber; the Campaign Chamber (established in the seventeenth century); the Pantry Chamber; the Treasury Chamber, dealing with the private as distinct from the public treasury; the Privy Chamber.

The last named, called in Turkish *Hass-oda,* was the highest in rank and nearest to the sultan. Its numbers varied between thirty and forty, and included several high dignitaries, such as the *Silihdar-aga,* the sword-bearer, and the stirrupholders, and the agas of the turban, the key, the napkin, and the ewer. The first four in rank were called the audience agas.

The pages of the *Hass-oda* were a hand-picked *corps d'élite,* at the summit of a vast organization with a complex system of training and promotion. From among their numbers the Sultans chose men for appointment to the highest posts in the central and provincial government.

Some idea of the education and career of the palace cadets may be obtained from Ottaviano Bon:

> It now remayneth, that I say somewhat of those Youths which are kept in better fashion in the Serraglio, for the King and Countreyes Service, brought up in Learning, in the knowledge of the Lawes, and in Military Exercises, that they may bee able to performe those things, which belong to the Government of the whole Empire. And albeit for the most part these are Christian Captives and Renegado's, yet there are some Naturall born Turkes amongst them. . . .

They have Roomes, which the Turkes call Oda's, but we may more properly (in regard of the use they are put unto) call them Schooles; of which there are foure, the one taking Degrees from the other. Now into the first they all come, when they are but children, where the Primarie Precept they learne is Silence; then their personall Positures, betokening singular Reverence to the King; which is, that they hold downe their heads and looke downwards, holding their hands before them joyned across. . . .

Then (by a white Eunuch who is chiefe over all the other Masters and Ushers) they are set to learne to write and reade, and to practise the Turkish Tongue; and are taught their prayers . . . in the Arabian tongue. . . . Now, for the most part, they all stay about five or six yeeres in this Schoole, and such as are dull and hard of apprehension stay longer.

From this Oda they are removed to the second, where (by more learned Tutors than the former) they are taught the Persian, Arabian, and Tartarian tongues, and take great paines in reading divers Authors, that they may be the better able to speake the Turkish elegantly . . . and indeed there is found a great difference betweene their speech, and that of the vulgar sort.

Here also they begin to learne to wrestle, to shoot in a Bow, to throw the Mace, to tosse the Pike, to handle their Weapons, to runne, &c. . . .

They spend other five or sixe yeeres likewise in this Odah from the which (being become men, strong, and fit for any thing) they are removed to the third Odah, where (forgetting nothing of what they learned before, but rather bettering themselves) they also learne to sit a Horse, and to be quick and nimble in the Warres. Moreover, every one of them (according to his inclination and disposition) shall learne a Trade, necessary for the Service of the Kings person. . . .

Here also the Eunuches, their tutors, make great tryall of their constancie in Religion, searching (as farre as in them lyes) their hearts, to see how they stand affected to Turcisme: For the time growing neere, wherein they are to passe to the fourth Odah, which is the chiefest and last, and from which they are called to businesse of great import; they would not then have them at all remember that they were formerly Christians, or to have any desire imaginable to turne to their first beliefe; lest that they should, by some strategems and politike carriage, prove disadvantageous to the Turkish Empire. So then, all possible proofe and triall being made, and they found to bee strongly perswaded in themselves of the truth of that Religion, they then are preferred to the fourth Odah where they are once more registered: For all they which are of the third Odah are not translated to the fourth at one and the same time, but only such as have gone through all the Degrees in the three former, and are become fit for Service: And there is an Account kept apart of them, which come into this fourth Odah, for they are immediately ordayned for the Grand Signiors owne Service, and have their pay encreased, some more and some lesse, unto eight Aspers per diem, and their habits changed from Cloth to Silke, and Cloth of Gold of great price. . . .

Now out of these young men of the fourth Oda (after they have finished the appointed terme of yeeres, and have beene well instructed in all things as aforesaid) the Grand Signior chooseth his Agha's, which are his Gentlemen and serve him only. . . .

The Grand Signior having bestowed . . . places upon them, they leave the Serraglio, and carrie with them all their estates, both money and goods: and often-times take with them other young men of the other Odahs, which are let go through their owne hastinesse, and great importunitie, not willing to stay out their time; but, losing the King's favour are content with small pay and lesser reputation, to goe along with the said Aghas. . . .

They which succeed in preferment, those that are gone out of the Serraglio upon the aforesaid employments; are (as the custome commandeth) such as are next in yeeres unto them, and of the longest standing: neither can this course be altered, unlesse by some sinister accident, or eville behaviour they faile thereof: So that it is alwaies knowne amongst themselves, who is next capable of publique employment; nay, the businesse is so orderly carried, and their course so regular, that even they of the third Odah doe know what their future fortunes will bee, if they live to enjoy them: And indeed all of them live in hope, and desire that the Grand Signior would often be pleased to send them abroad, that so they may the sooner be out of their hard service in the Serraglio, and enter into the state of ample government. . . . It is no marvel then the Turkish officers are so often changed, seeing that every Grand Signior hath so many servants of his own, that seek for advancement. . . .

They all strive to gaine the love of the Capee Agha; that he may bee a Protector and Patron unto them, and that, when they are absent, he may possesse the Grand Signior with a good opinion of them; for they know he is very powerful with him, being the chiefest in the Serraglio, and alwaies neerest to the King.

Between the Middle Gate and the Gate of Felicity stood the *Divanhane,* the Council House, where the Imperial Council, the *Divan-i Hümayun,* met in the famous Dome Chamber. Ottaviano Bon describes the meetings in these terms:

The Divan dayes are foure in the Weeke; viz. Saturday, Sunday, Munday and Tuesday, upon which dayes, the Chiefe Vizir, with all the rest of the Vizirs; the two Cadileschers [*Kadiaskers*] of Graecia and Natolia (which are the Chiefe over all the Cadies of those two Provinces ...); the three Defterdars, (whose charge is to gather in the Kings Revenues, and likewise to pay all the Souldiers, and others which have any stipend due unto them:) the Reiskitawb (which is the chancellor) the Nishawngee (that is, hee which sighneth the Commandments and Letters with the Grand Signiors marke); the Secretaries of all the Bashawes, and other great men; a great number of Clerkes or Scriveners, which are alwayes at hand attending at the doore of the Divan; The Chiaush Bashee, who all that while that he is in the Serraglio, carrieth a silver staffe in his hand; and many Chiaushes also to attend, that at the command of the Vizir, they may bee ready to bee dispatched with such order as shall bee given them by him, to what place, or to whom soever; For, they are those which are employed in Ambassies, in ordinary Messages, to summon men to appeare before the Justice, to keepe close Prisoners, and in fine to performe all businesses of that nature. All which aforesaid Officers, from the highest to the lowest, are to be at the Divan by breake of day.

The Vizirs being come into the Divan, doe sit within at the further end thereof, with their faces towards the doore, upon a bench which joyneth to the wall, every one in his place as hee is in degree, sitting all at the right hand of the chiefe Vizir (for with the laity the left is counted the upper hand, but with the clergy the right); and on his left hand upon the same bench doe sit the two Cadeleschers, first hee of Grecia, as being the more noble and famous Province; and then hee of Natolia. And on the right side at the coming in at the doore: doe sit the three Defterdars, who have behind them (in the aforesayd roome,

82

which is divided with a wooden rayle) all the sayd Clerks or Scriveners who sit upon the ground, with Paper and Pennes in their hands, being ready to write whatsoever is commanded them. And on the other side (over against the Defterdars) doth sit the Nishawngee, with his Pen in his hand: having his Officers round about him. The Reiskitawb, for the most part, stands close by the Vizir, for he takes his advice in many occurents. And in the middest of the roome doe stand all such as require audience of the Bench.

Now being all come together, and every man set in his own place, forthwith the Petitioners begin their suites, one by one (who have no need of Attorneyes, though oftentimes they procure the help of a Chiaush, for every man may speake for himselfe) referring themselves to the judgement and sentence of the Chiefe Vizir, who (if hee please) may end all: for the other Bashawes doe not speake, but only hearken and attend till such time as he shall referre any thing to their arbitriment, as oftentime hee doth, for hee having once understood the substance onely of the Cause (to free himselfe from too much trouble) remits the deciding of the greatest part to others; As for example, if it bee appertayning to the Civill Law, hee remits it to the Cadeleschers. If it bee of Accounts, to the Defterdars. If of Falshood (as counterfeiting the Marke or such like) to the Nishawngee. If concerning Merchants, or Merchandizes (wherein there may bee any great difficultie) to some one of the other Bashawes which sit by him; so that after this manner he doth exceedingly ease himselfe of so great a burthen, which otherwise hee alone should bee enforced to undergoe; reserving onely to himselfe what hee thinketh to bee of greatest import and consequence; and the like course doth the Caimekam take in his absence. And on this wise they spend the time untill it bee Noone; at which houre (one of the Sewers being appointed to bee there present) the Chiefe Vizir commands that the Dinner bee brought in; and immediately all the common people depart. . . .

Dinner being ended, the chiefe Vizir spendeth some small time about generale Affaires, and taking Counsell together (if he pleaseth and thinketh it fit) with the other Bashawes; at last, he determineth and resolveth of all within himselfe, and prepareth to goe in unto the King; It being the ordinarie custome so to doe, in two of the foure Divan dayes, that is, upon Sunday, and upon Tuesday; to render an account unto his Majestie of all such businesses as hee hath dispatched. And to this end, the Grand Signior (after hee hath dined also) repayreth unto his Chamber of Audience, and being set downe upon a Sofa, sendeth the Capi Agha (which hath in his hand a Silver staff) to call first the Cadileschers, who immediately rise up out of their places, and having bowed to the chiefe Vizir, they depart, being accompanied with the sayd Capi Agha, and Chiaush Bashee, who go before them with their Silver staves in their hands, and so they goe in unto the King, to give account and make him acquainted with what hath passed concerning their Charge, and so they being dismissed (for that day) they goe directly home to their owne Houses.

Next after them are called the Defterdars, who in the same manner are brought unto the King, but the chief Defterdar is only permitted to speake; and having dispatched, they take leave, and give place to the Vizirs, who are called last of all, and goe together in a ranke, one after another, the Chiefe Vizir being formost, ushered along by the two aforesayd Silver staves. And being come before the presence of the Grand Signior, they stand all on one side of the room, with their hands before them, holding downe their heads, in token of Humilitie; and so none but the Chiefe Vizir speaketh, and

gives an account of what hee thinketh fit, delivering his Me-
morials, or Arzes [*Arz*—petition, deposition], one by one, the
which the King having read, the Vizir taketh them, and having put them into a little crimson Sattin bagge, he most humbly
layeth them downe againe before his Majestie, who afterwards
causeth his Hattee-humawyoon [*Hatt-i Hümayun*—Imperial
rescript] to be drawn for the performance of what the Arzes
did require. If the Grand Signior demand no further of him
(the other Bashawes not having spoken one word all this
while) they all depart and take horse at the second Gate;
and being accompanied by divers men of quality (who, to
insinuate into their favours, do wait upon them) besides a great
many of their owne people, every one goes to his own house.
The Chief Vizir, for his greater grace and honour, hath commonly about an hundred Chiaushes on horseback, who bring
him to his home, and so the Divan is ended for that day, it
being about three hours after noon; but upon such days as they
have no audience of the King, they dispatch sooner. And what
hath been said of the Chiefe Vizir, the same also is to be understood of the Caimekam in his absence.

It is to be noted that sometimes also the Agha of the
Janizaries, and the Captaine Bashaw come to the Divan, when
they are at home in Constantinople, and have businesse to doe
there: but the Captaine Bashaw only doth goe in unto the King
(which also may not be but in companie of the other Bashawes) to acquaint his Highnesse with the state and affaires of
the Arsenal and Armado; his place in the Divan is upon the
same Bench, but yet hee sitteth last of all the Bashawes, unlesse hee be one of the Viziers (as it is often seene) and then
hee sitteth second, or third, or fourth, as he is in degree by
election: but the Agha of the Janizaries doth not sit in Divan,
but sitteth under the open Gallerie on the right hand, within

the second Gate; and if so bee it so fall out, upon some extraordinarie businesse, that he bee to goe in unto the King, then he goeth first of all others; and being come out againe from him, he sitteth downe againe in his place, until the Divan be ended. He is the last that departeth of all the great men, and is attended on by a great many Churbegees and Janizaries unto his Serraglio, where he and many of them do live together.

The Grand Signior's Predecessors were alwaies wont to come, and this man sometimes commeth privately by an upper way to a certaine little window which looketh into the Divan, right over the head of the Chiefe Vizir, and there sitteth with a Lattice before him, that he may not be seene, to heare and see what is done in the Divan; and especially at such times when he is to give audience to any Ambassadour from a great Prince, to see him eate, and heare him reason with the Bashawes: and by this his coming to that window, the Chiefe Vizir (who alwaies standeth in jeopardy of losing his head, upon any displeasure of the Grand Signior) is enforced to carrie himself very uprightly and circumspectly in the managing of affairs, whilst he sits in Divan; though at other times his hands are open to bribery, and carry businesses as he pleaseth.

In early times the sultans used to preside in person over the meetings of the Divan, but ceased to do so when they adopted the pomp and ceremony of the older Islamic imperial courts. Mehemmed II was the first to give up this function, relinquishing it to the Grand Vizier. According to an anecdote related by later Ottoman historians, the reason was that one day a peasant with a grievance walked into the assembled council and said: "Which one of you is the Sultan? I have a complaint." The Sultan was offended, and the Grand Vizier Gedik Ahmed Pasha seized the opportunity to suggest that he might avoid such embarrassments by not appearing at the Divan in person. Instead, he could observe the proceedings from behind a grille or screen. This practice was indeed followed until the time of Süleyman the Magnificent, who ceased to attend the meetings of the Divan even in this form. Thereafter, the Sultan left it to the Grand Vizier, who had emerged as the dominant figure in the government of the Ottoman Empire, presiding over both the civil and military—though not the religious—branches of the administration.

The title and function of vizier (Arabic *wazir*) have a long history in the Islamic world, and go back to the classical days of the caliphs in Baghdad. In the Ottoman state vizier was originally a military title, given to army commanders, and was given to the senior officers of the state under the sultan. There were several viziers, the first among them being the grand vizier, who became in effect the chief minister of state. In the *kanun* of Mehemmed the Conqueror he is already called the "absolute representative" of the sultan. The lesser viziers were called dome viziers because they shared the privilege of attending the meetings of the Imperial Divan in the Dome Chamber.

Until the Conquest, the grand vizier was usually free, drawn from the Muslim nobility. The first to emerge from the slave household was Mahmud Pasha, a former Balkan Christian who held office from 1453 to 1466; thereafter the grand viziers were almost without exception men of Christian origin, recruited by the *devshirme* and trained in the imperial schools and palace.

One of the most distinguished holders of the office in the sixteenth century was Lutfi Pasha, statesman and historian, who served as grand vizier to Süleyman the Magnificent and who, in addition to his high state office, had the more intimate and dangerous privilege of being the Sultan's brother-in-law. Of obscure Albanian origin, he was recruited into the Ottoman service by the *devshirme,* and graduated from the palace school into the palace service, where he was successively *chokadar, müteferrika,* chief taster, chief gate-warden, and imperial standard-bearer. He was then posted governor of the Sanjak of Kastamonu, in Asia Minor, and rose in the provincial service to the rank of governor general of Karaman. He took part in several of the major military campaigns of Selim I in the East and of Süleyman in Europe. He became a dome vizier in 1534 and was appointed grand vizier in 1539: he held office until 1541 when he was summarily dismissed for speaking rudely to his wife, the Sultan's sister. He then retired with a pension to his estate near Dimetoka, where he devoted his remaining years to scholarship and history.

Lutfi Pasha wrote a number of works, including a history of the Ottoman Empire up to and including his own time, and a little book on the Grand Vizierate entitled *Asafname,* the *Book of Asaph,* after the Biblical personage who, according to Muslim tradition, was the vizier of King Solomon, and the model of the wise and loyal minister. When Lutfi Pasha became a vizier, he tells us, he found the affairs of the Imperial Divan in confusion and disorder, and did his best to set it right during his seven years in the vizierate. Thereafter he withdrew to a life of study and contemplation:

> The kingdom of this mortal world is swift in passing and full of death. It is better to find wise but not heedless repose

in the corner of leisure and the enjoyment of gardens and meadows. May God, from Whom we seek aid, and in Whom we trust, secure the laws and foundations of the House of Osman from the fear and peril of fate and from the evil eye of the foe, amen.

To make things easier for his successors, Lutfi Pasha felt it his duty to set down, in four chapters, some advice and guidance, based on his own experience, for the proper conduct of this great office, the highest to which a subject can aspire. The first and most important chapter deals with the qualities desirable in a grand vizier, and the proper way for him to conduct himself in his dealings with the sultan on the one hand and with the subjects on the other.

First and foremost, he who is grand vizier must have no private purposes or spite. Everything he does should be for God and in God and for the sake of God, for above this there is no higher rank to which he could attain. He should tell the Sultan the truth, without fear or concealment. . . . The secrets which the grand vizier shares with the Sultan must be withheld not only from outsiders, but even from the other viziers. . . .

The grand vizier should speak to the sovereign, without hesitation, of what is necessary in the affairs of both religion and the state, and should not be held back by fear of dismissal. It is better to be dismissed and respected among men than to render dishonest service.

The vizier should limit the demands of the state on the subject, and should preserve the sultan from greed for money and from the harmful results to which it leads. The property of the subject must be respected, "for the summary annexation of the property of the people to the property of the sovereign is a sign of decay in the state." The grand vizier himself must be pious, accessible, and scrupulously honest:

> The grand vizier should celebrate the five daily prayers, with his suite, in his house. His door should be open, he himself easy of access, and as far as is possible without dishonor, he should try to give satisfaction. He should take care not to allow any scoundrels or thieves to buy their way with gifts. For officers of the state, corruption is a disease without remedy. . . . Beware, beware of corruption, O God, save us from it!

After this sudden note of passion, Lutfi Pasha observes, more practically, that the income of the grand vizier should be enough to preserve him from this danger:

> The occupant of the grand vizierate holds an appanage with an income of 1,200,000 aspers, which by good management he can bring up to near 2,000,000; together with some 2–300,000 aspers worth of cloths and horses from the Kurdish and other powerful emirs, his total annual income must be about 2,400,000 aspers. By the grace of almighty God, this is, in the Ottoman state, a sufficient bounty. I myself used to spend 1,500,000 aspers a year on the needs of my kitchen and my staff, and 500,000 on charity, leaving another 400,000 or 500,000 in my treasury. . . . Greed is an evil way, that has no end; contentment is a treasure with many benefits, that doth not fade away.

The grand vizier would have no time for pleasure or entertainment, but must devote himself entirely to the service of the state.

After having attained this post, that which becomes him is

silence and austerity. As far as possible, he should strive for the salvation of his soul and the betterment of the world.

Lutfi Pasha was also anxious about the cost of living and the prevention of profiteering:

> The control of prices is an important public responsibility, and the grand vizier must devote special care to it. It is not right if one high official is a rice-dealer or if the house of another is a drug-store. The fixing of prices is in the interests of the poor.

The grand vizier must exercise careful control over government appointments and promotions, which should be solely by merit. He should maintain discipline and respect the order of precedence and seniority. He should submit to no outside influence or pressure, but follow his judgment—though, of course, the final responsibility belongs to the sultan, who must from time to time be reminded of this fact:

> The grand vizier in speaking to the world-protecting Sultan should repeatedly say: "My Emperor, I have cast the yoke off my neck. On the Day of Judgment henceforth you will answer."

The three remaining chapters deal with the armed forces, the treasury, and the peasantry. "The Sultanate stands on its treasury. The treasury stands on good management. By tyranny it falls."

The grand vizier presided over a hierarchy and staff of civilian officials, grouped into two main services—the chancery and the finance office. These were for the most part freeborn Muslims, usually Turkish, and in time came to constitute a quasi-hereditary caste, with skills and mysteries of their own. They were in the main recruited from established bureaucratic families, and seem to have had many links with the religious classes, who were responsible for their education. They went to mosque primary schools and Muslim religious seminaries until the age of about sixteen or seventeen, when they were placed, usually by a relative, in a government office as apprentices, to learn the work and enter on the ladder of promotion. Many of the Muslim-born descendants of the Slaves of the Gate, themselves excluded from that service, found a career in the bureaucracy. The higher posts in the bureaucracy were frequently held by members of the religious classes and at times the senior bureaucratic and religious offices seem to be part of the same *cursus honorum*.

The officer who, under the general supervision of the grand vizier, was in charge of the finances was the chief defterdar, or keeper of the register. In the *kanun* of Mehemmed the Conqueror he is named immediately after the grand vizier, and was comparable with him in status. He had the right of personal access to the sultan, who, according to the *kanun,* rose to his feet to greet him. The chief defterdar presided over a hierarchy of lesser defterdars, with a recognized and established ladder of promotion. From the time of Bayezid II the chief defterdar was mainly concerned with Rumelia; a second was placed in charge of Anatolia, and a third added in the sixteenth century. All three were members of the Divan, and were usually drawn from the class of the ulema.

The head of the corps of ulema, the chief mufti of the capital, did not attend the Divan. Other ulema of high rank did, however. Immediately following the chief mufti in rank were the military judges (*ḳadi-asḳer*) of Rumelia and Anatolia, the supreme judicial authorities of the Empire; both were full members of the Divan. So too was the *nishanji,* whose primary duty was to affix the sultan's sign manual, and who was also, in effect, a kind of chancellor, with important legal powers. The *nishanji* had to approve the legality of documents before affixing the sign manual; he was an authority on the old *ḳanuns* of the Empire, and was responsible for the drafting of new ones. Until the early sixteenth century the *nishanjis* were always drawn from the ulema class; thereafter they were from the Divan secretariat, and suffered a diminution of status and authority.

During the sixteenth century, a new functionary appeared in the form of the "chief of the scribes," *reis ül-ḳüttab,* usually called *Reis Efendi.* He was chief state secretary and head of the chancery, under the general authority of the grand vizier. His duties thus included the conduct of relations with foreign states, in which he was assisted by the chief dragoman to the Divan—the *Terjüman-bashi.* The dragomans, or interpreters, were almost invariably Christians, in the earlier period usually of European origin, and they played a role of growing importance. Later this post was monopolized by a group of aristocratic Greek families residing in the Phanar district of Istanbul.

Neither the chief secretary nor the chief dragoman were full members of the Divan; together with other functionaries of similar rank, such as the chief pursuivant and chief chamberlain, they waited in attendance, and participated when called upon.

The armed forces were represented at the Divan by two

persons, the aga of the janissaries, for the army, and the grand admiral (*ḳapudan pasha*) for the fleet. These could, however, only be members if they had attained the rank of vizier. For the provinces, there were the two governors general (*beyler-bey*) of Rumelia and Anatolia, who attended the Divan when they were in the capital. Former holders of these two offices, the highest in the provincial administration, were also members of the Divan.

Until the mid-seventeenth century, the Imperial Divan was the center of the government of the Ottoman Empire. Its members, representing chancery, finance, law, religion, and the armed forces, met regularly and decided on all important questions of state. To implement their decisions, they had a large and well organized staff of civil servants, divided into departments, each with its own hierarchy and ladder of promotion. The military, religious, and financial chiefs had their own separate establishments; the rest formed the Divan secretariat which was presided over by the grand vizier, and divided into a number of departments dealing with different branches of central and provincial government.

In early Ottoman times the grand vizier had no official residence, but used to rent a mansion in the neighborhood of the palace, where he transacted some business and received some callers; the reception quarters of this house came to be known as *Pasha Kapisi*—the pasha's gate, in contrast to the Imperial Gate of the sultan's palace. To deal with business left over by the Imperial Divan, the practice grew of holding an afternoon meeting in the grand vizier's house, after the *Iḳindi,* the afternoon prayer. This meeting—the *Iḳindi* Divan, as it was called—came to meet regularly five days a week and gradually took over a large part of the business of the Imperial Divan.

The transfer of the center of government from the Imperial Divan to the Grand Vizierate was formalized in 1654, when Sultan Mehemmed IV presented the vizier with a building, which served him both as an official residence and office. It was to this that the term *Pasha Kapisi* now came to be applied. The use of such terms as gate, door, and threshold to denote the seat of government is very ancient in the Middle East, and is attested in the Ottoman state from early times. Up to the seventeenth century, the term "gate" and its equivalents were used of the sultan's palace or Divan. After this date the term came to be used more frequently of the grand vizier's establishment, now generally recognized, at home and abroad, as the real seat of government. In the eighteenth century it became known as the *Bab-i Ali,* usually translated as the Sublime Porte.

V. The City

A TURKISH HISTORIAN tells us that in 1659, when the Ottoman ambassador to the Mogul court in Delhi returned to Istanbul, the Sultan asked him what was the most remarkable thing he had seen during his journey to the fabulous land of India. The ambassador replied that his safe departure from there and his return to "this place that is like paradise" was the most wonderful of all his experiences.

In this answer which, we are told, greatly pleased the Sultan, there was no doubt something of courtly flattery; but it does reflect a genuine sentiment of pride and love which the Ottomans felt for their magnificent capital city. The seventeenth-century poet Nabi in a compendium of good advice—better advice than verse—addressed to his son, includes a eulogy of Istanbul that gives some expression to this feeling:

> There is no place where knowledge and learning
> Find so ready a welcome as Istanbul.

No city has eaten the fruits of the garden of art
So richly as the city of Istanbul.

May God cause Istanbul to flourish
For it is the home of all great affairs.

Birthplace and school of famous men,
The nursery of many nations,

Whatever men of merit there may be
All win their renown in Istanbul.

There every perfection finds its measure,
There every talent attains its value.

There are the ranks of glory and honour
Anywhere else life is frittered away.

. . .

The heavens may turn about the earth as they will
They will find no city like Istanbul.

Drawing and painting, writing and gilding
Achieve beauty and grace in Istanbul.

However many different arts there may be
All find brilliance and lustre in Istanbul.

Because its beauty is so rare a sight
The sea has clasped it in an embrace.

All the arts and all the crafts
Find honor and glory in Istanbul.

Having celebrated Istanbul as a place of opportunity and
a center of art and learning, Nabi goes on to speak of the
simpler pleasures of the city by the sea:

Apart from the rest, what joy and delight
To float on the face of the sea,

To ascend the throne like Süleyman
And lord it over sea and air,

Leaning on a cushion,
Looking in the silver mirror,

Where in faultless order are combined
The sounds of music, the lyre of joy.

Floating along, effortlessly wafted by the breeze, the poet
beholds the splendid skyline of the city:

Aya Sofya, the wonder of the ages
Its dome the eighth of the heavenly spheres—

We have not seen its peer in any land
It has none, save perhaps in Paradise.

The threshold of the Ottoman Sultanate
The delight of the imperial realm.

In this life-giving place
Whatever you wish is forthcoming.

Whatever thing may come into your mind
The finest and best of it is here.

Bey, Pasha, Efendi, Chelebi,
Here are the choicest of them all.

Soldiers and scholars and knights
Here are the kings of them all.

Here every problem of the world finds solution
Here every effort achieves its goal

Then, with that practical common sense that rarely deserts
the Turk, Nabi remarks:

Were it not for all kinds of diseases

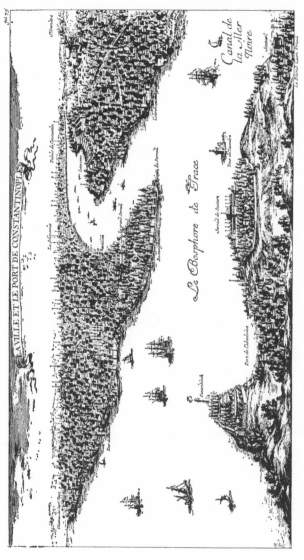

The Town and Port of Istanbul (at that time called Constantinople).
Reproduced from G. J. Grelot's *Relation nouvelle d'un voyage de Constantinople* (Paris, 1680).
Courtesy Dumbarton Oaks Research Library and Collection of Harvard University, Washington, D.C.

> Were it not for the accursed plague
>
> Who would ever leave this place like paradise
> This grief-dispelling city?
>
> If its weather were only more equable
> Who would ever look at any other place?

But all the same

> There is no land or city that is like it
> No place to live that can compare with it.

When Mehemmed the Conqueror entered the conquered city of Constantinople, it was little more than a ruin, in which the processes of decline and decay had been brought to an accelerated climax by the swift ordeal of battle and capture. Of the fifty thousand or so inhabitants that remained in the Byzantine city, the survivors of the final struggle became the slaves of the victors and took the road to Edirne, to the slave market of the Turkish capital. Constantinople was left empty and desolate.

But the new masters were not content to rule over a city of ruins and empty spaces. In the words of the *gazi* chronicler Ashikpashazade:

> When Sultan Mehemmed Khan Gazi had captured Istanbul, he made Süleyman Bey city commandant. Then he sent his servants to all his lands, to say: "Whoever wishes, let him come, and let him become owner of houses, vineyards and gardens in Istanbul." And they gave them to all who came.
>
> This, however, was not enough to repopulate the city. This time, therefore, the Sultan gave orders to despatch families,

both rich and poor, from every province. The Sultan's servants were sent with orders to the Kadis and commandants of every province, and in accordance with their orders conscribed and brought very many families. Houses were also given to these new arrivals, and this time the city began to be repeopled. . . .

They began to build mosques. Some of them built dervish convents, some of them private houses, and the city returned to its previous state. . . .

The sultan . . . built eight medreses with a great cathedral mosque in their midst, and facing the mosque a fine hospice and a hospital, and at the side of the eight medreses he built eight more small medreses, to house the students. Apart from this, he had a fine mausoleum built over the grave of the holy Eyyub-i Ensari, with a hospice, a medrese, and a mosque nearby.

Ashikpashazade's description of Mehemmed's policy of re-settlement is confirmed by many other sources and documents. It was not limited to Turks or Muslims. Greeks and other Christians were permitted—in some cases were encouraged—to settle in the city, and Jews were invited or directed to Istanbul from other Ottoman lands, and beyond. A document of 1478, listing the numbers of households in Istanbul and Galata, gives some measure of the progress that had been made. It records 8,951 Muslims, 3,151 Greek, 1,647 Jewish, 267 Crimean, 372 Armenian, 384 Karamanli, and 31 gypsy households in Istanbul; 535 Muslim, 592 Greek, 332 Frankish, and 62 Armenian households in Galata—a probable total population of between seventy and eighty thousand, of whom about a tenth lived in the Christian settlement of Galata, and the rest in the old city of Istanbul. By the time of Süleyman the Magnificent the population had risen to at least half a million, and in 1593 an English traveler, John Sanderson, cites a local informant, giving the figure of 1,231,207, made up as follows:

In Constantinople ar resident:

Viziers (I say Viseroyes)	6
Every vizier hath but 1000 aspers a day pay.	
The Grete Turke aloweth himselfe but 1001.	
Cadyes, that is Judges, of the learned of their religion,	4
Thes 10 sitt in divan to judge all causes.	
Muftie, the cheefe judge of thier religion and highe priest	1
Defterdare is treasurer. Emrahur Bassie master of the horsses. Janisari Aga, captine of janisaris. Chaous Aga. Capigie Aga. Spahie Aga. Bustangie Basshi. Captain Bashawe. Capi Aga.	
Piekes [*peyk*], pentioners about his person	300
Solacks [*solak*], his footmen	300
Falconers, dwarfs, and dome [dumb] men	300
Whores of all sorts, at least	1,000
Chahouses [*Chaush*], that is officers or sargients belonging to his courts	1,600
Capogies, that is porters to his gates (70 waits every ordinary day), of them	700
Spahies, which ar his gentillmen, I say horsemen	30,000
Janisaries, to say footmen, common soldiers	24,000
Topgies, gunners aboute his great artilarie	3,000
Jamoglains, youths to make janisaries	20,000
	——————
	81,207

Other Turks, dwellers in the citie (besides women and children)	200,000
Christians of all sorts and contryes, at least	200,000
Jues in and neare about the citie, at least	150,000
Women and children of all sorts, Christians, Jues, Turks etc.	600,000
	1,231,207

Ottoman Istanbul was a great and thriving city, with a diverse and active population. Few Greeks had remained after the conquest, but many had returned, and others had come to join them from all parts of the Empire, forming a flourishing community under the leadership of their own patriarch. The Jews too, already present in the Byzantine city, increased greatly in numbers, especially from the end of the fifteenth century, when many of them came from Spain, Portugal, and other European countries, seeking a refuge from Christian oppression under the tolerant rule of the sultans. In accordance with Islamic and Ottoman practice, Christians and Jews alike enjoyed freedom of worship, and were accorded a large measure of communal autonomy. In the European quarters on the eastern bank of the Golden Horn, Italian and, later, other Western merchants established their warehouses, their offices, and their homes. Most important of all was the steadily growing Turkish-speaking Muslim majority, recruited by conversion, by assimilation, and above all by settlement.

The Turks who entered Constantinople were not the simple barbarians depicted by some Western writers, but the heirs and carriers of an old and high civilization—that of classical Islam, to which they themselves had added a not inconsiderable contribution. Seljuk and Ottoman architecture already had an old-established and distinguished tradition, and the new masters of Aya Sofya possessed—fortunately for posterity—the skill and resources to preserve and embellish it. Islam disapproves of the representation of the human form, and so the Turks concealed the famous mosaics under a grey limewash—though this does not seem to have happened until centuries after the conquest. The structure, however, was maintained and strengthened. Mehemmed the Conqueror added a minaret, and supported the south wall with a great buttress; Selim II added two more minarets, and two buttresses on the north wall. His son Murad III completed the four minarets that now stand at the four corners of the building, and carried out extensive repairs and renovations in the whole building.

Apart from the palace, the most important new building erected in the city by the conquerors was the great mosque of Sultan Mehemmed, built on the fourth hill in the years 1462–70, together with its dependent complex of academic and other buildings. It was destroyed in an earthquake in 1766. It was natural that the new emperor in the city should try to vie with Aya Sofya by erecting a new monument to his own conquering faith. But the Conqueror's mosque was not only a place of worship; it was also a center of higher education. The eight *medreses,* with their eight dependent dormitory buildings, formed a kind of university city, in which theology, law, medicine, and the rest of the traditional Islamic sciences were taught. It was known, from its pattern, as *Sahn-i Seman,* the Court of Eight, and remained one of the chief centers of learning, despite the subsequent foundation of many other medreses. Sultans, ministers, and other men of piety and property vied with one another in founding and endowing mosques and medreses.

During the lifetime of the Conqueror, several of his chief ministers also founded mosques in the city, some of which, notably those of the Grand Vizier Mahmud Pasha (1464) and of another vizier called Murad Pasha (1466) remain standing. The example of the first Sultan in Istanbul was followed by his successors. Bayezid II built a great mosque, near the Bazaars (1501–1506). Another, on the fifth hill, above the Greek quarter called Phanar, bears the name of Selim I.

The first three sultans in the new capital all made their contributions to the revival and growth of the city. It was, however, under Süleyman the Magnificent that the city reached the peak of its splendor. The center of a vast, rich, and expanding empire, it offered resources and opportunities to artists and writers, scholars, soldiers, and statesmen, merchants and entrepreneurs, who thronged to the new imperial capital from all the far-flung provinces of the Empire, and beyond them.

Perhaps the finest Ottoman monument in the city is the Süleymaniye, crowning the summit of the highest hill. The mosque, with its dependent colleges and foundations, and with the mausoleum of Süleyman in its court, was built in 1550–56; it was one of the supreme masterpieces of Sinan (*ca.* 1489–1588), by common consent the greatest of Ottoman architects. Of Christian parentage, Sinan was born in Kayseri, in central Anatolia, and in 1512 was recruited by the *devshirme* levy into the Ottoman service. Trained in the palace school in Istanbul, he graduated into the corps of Janissaries, and took part in both the European and Persian campaigns. He soon rose in rank, becoming first an infantry and then a technical officer, and distinguished himself in bridge-building and other forms of military engineering. Under Süleyman and Selim II, he was exclusively occupied with commissions from the sultans and high dignitaries of the Empire, from 1539 with the title of chief architect (*mimar-bashi*). An autobiographical fragment dictated by Sinan lists 312 buildings erected by him, including great and small mosques, schools and colleges, tombs and mausolea, palaces, hospitals, hospices and caravanserais, bridges, aqueducts, magazines, and bathhouses.

The structure and decoration of the Süleymaniye mosque, built a century after the conquest of Istanbul, illustrate at the same time the enrichment of Turkish Islam by earlier streams of tradition, and the essential and distinctive originality of its own religious and aesthetic life. Though the mosque reflects the convergence of both Persian and Byzantine influences, there is something new, different, and characteristically Ottoman in the harmonious contrast of minarets and dome, in the lightness of touch in the use of the dome itself, and in the spacious and elegant interior.

Its most striking feature, the great central dome, obviously owes much to the example of Aya Sofya, but the Ottoman architect made several significant changes. In Muslim communal prayer, the worshippers stand side by side, in long rows, facing the *Kibla* which shows the direction of Mecca. They are led by the Imam, whom they must follow exactly, and there is special merit in being in the front row. Unlike the church, the mosque is therefore usually planned in breadth, with naves parallel to the *Kibla* wall. In the earlier Arab mosques, there was usually a wide chamber opening on a great open court. In the colder climate of Turkey, however, an enclosed and roofed place was needed, to shelter worshippers from the wind and the rain, while still allowing the lateral extension needed for Muslim worship.

In the Süleymaniye mosque, the central cupola is still buttressed by two half-domes, but these are no longer supported by great semicircular niches as in Aya Sofya. By finding another solution to the problem of giving strength and balance to the central dome, Sinan was able to clear the central space under it of pillars and other encumbrances. The disposition in breadth and the elimination of the central supports gave room for wide rows of worshippers, with a clear and unbroken view of the Imam and the *Kibla*.

The seventeenth-century Ottoman writer Evliya Chelebi describes its construction and appearance in these terms:

Süleyman having assembled all the thousands of perfect masters in architecture, building, stone-hewing, and marble-cutting, who were found in the dominions of the house of Osman, three whole years were employed in laying the foundations. The workmen penetrated so far into the earth, that the sound of their pickaxes was heard by the bull that bears up the world at the bottom of the earth. In three more years the foundations reached the face of the earth; but in the ensuing year the building was suspended, and the workmen were employed in sawing and cutting various coloured stones for the building above the foundations. In the following year the Mihrab [prayer-niche] was fixed ... and the walls, which reached the vault of heaven, were completed, and on those four solid foundations they placed its lofty dome. . . . Besides the square piers which support it, there are, on the right and left sides, four porphyry columns, each of which is worth ten times the amount of the tribute from Egypt. . . . On the side next to the Mihrab, and on that opposite to it, the dome is joined by the two semi-domes, which do not, however, rest on those columns, as the architect was afraid of over-loading them. Sinan opened windows on every side to give light to the mosque. . . . On the right and left of the Mihrab there are spirally-twisted columns, which appear like the work of magic. There are also candlesticks of a man's stature, made of pure brass, and gilded with pure gold, which hold candles of camphorated bees'-wax, each 20 quintals in weight. . . . On both sides of the mosque there are benches, supported by low columns, one of which looks upon the sea, and the other on the market. When the mosque is very much crowded, many persons perform their devotions on these benches. There are also, round the cupola, within the mosque, two rows of galleries supported by columns, which, on the blessed nights, are lighted with lamps. The total number of the lamps is 22,000; and there are likewise some thousands of other ornaments suspended from the roof. There are windows on all the four sides of the mosque, through each of which refreshing breezes enter and revive the congregation; so that they seem to be enjoying eternal life in Paradise. . . .

The court of this mosque has three gates, to which there is an ascent and descent by three flights of steps. It is paved with white marble, and is as smooth and level as a carpet. . . . Over the windows on each side of this court there are texts from the Koran inscribed in white letters on blue tiles. The door opposite to the kibla [i.e. the north door] is the largest of all; it is of white marble, and has not its equal on earth for the beauty and skill with which it is carved and ornamented. . . . Over the sill of the door there are sculptured flowers and festoons of filigree work, interlaced with each other with a skill rivalling the art of Jemshid. On each side of this gate there are buildings four-stories high, containing chambers for the hour-cryers, porters and sextons. At the entrance of this gate there is a large circular block of red porphyry, which is unparalleled for its size and the fineness of its polish. . . .

On the pedestals of the columns round the four sides of this court there are brass plates, on which the dates of memorable events, such as great fires, earthquakes, revolts and tumults, are engraven. This mosque has four minarets, the galleries of which are ten in number, as a record that Sultan Süleyman Khan was the tenth Sultan of the House of Osman. The two minarets adjoining the body of the mosque have each three galleries, to which there is an ascent by a staircase of two hundred steps; the two minarets at the inner angles of the court are lower, and have but two galleries each. . . .

The outer court of this mosque is a large sandy level planted with cypresses, planes, willows, limes, and ashes; and surrounding three sides of the building. It has ten gates. . . . On this [the east] side the court [harem] is not enclosed by a wall, but merely by a low parapet, that the view of the city of Islambol may not be interrupted. There the congregation remains and enjoys a full view of the imperial palace, Scutari, the castle of the Bosphorus, Beshik-tash, Top-hane, Galata, Kasim Pasha, the Okmeydan, and the Golden Horn and the Bosphorus, traversed by a thousand boats and barges and other kinds of vessels—a spectacle not to be equalled in any other place in the world! The circumference of this outer court is one thousand paces. There is also a smaller court called the Pehlivan Demir meydani [i.e. wrestlers' iron ground] between this mosque and the walls of the old saray. It is a valley where wrestlers from all the convents exercise themselves when after-noon-prayer is over.

To the right and left of this mosque there are four great colleges for the education of jurists in the four sects, which are now filled with men of the most profound learning. There is likewise a school for instruction in the traditional law; a school for instruction in the recitation of chanting of the Koran; a college for the study of medicine; a school for chil-dren; a hospital, a refectory, an alms-house, a hospital for strangers, a karvansaray for travellers, a market for gold-smiths and button and book makers, a bath, with apartments for the students, and thousands of chambers for their servants; so that within the precincts of the mosque there are alto-gether not less than 1001 cupolas. Seen from Galata the Süley-maniye seems like one vast plain covered with lead. The whole number of servants attached to the mosque is three thousand. They are maintained by secure and liberal endowments, all the islands in the Aegean Sea, as Cos, Chios, and Rhodes hav-ing been settled on it by Sultan Süleyman. Its revenues are col-lected by five hundred men under the direction of the com-missioner. . . .

When it was finished, the architect Sinan said to the Sultan: "I have built for thee, O emperor, a mosque which will re-main on the face of the earth till the day of judgment; and when Hallaj Mansur comes, and rends Mount Demavand from its foundation, he will play at tennis with it and the cupola of this mosque." . . . The humble writer of these lines once him-self saw ten Frankish infidels skilful in geometry and archi-tecture, who, when the door-keeper had changed their shoes for slippers, and had introduced them into the mosque for the purpose of shewing it to them, laid their finger on their mouths, and each bit his finger from astonishment when they saw the minarets; but when they beheld the dome they tossed up their hats and cried Maria! Maria! and on observing the four arches which support the dome on which the date A.H. 944 [A.D. 1537] is inscribed, they could not find terms to express their admiration, and the ten, each laying his finger on his mouth, remained a full hour looking with astonishment on those arches. Afterwards, on surveying the exterior, the court, and its four minarets, six gates, its columns, arches and cupolas, they again took off their hats and went round the mosque bareheaded, that being their manner of testifying the greatest amazement. I asked their interpreter how they liked it, and one of them who was able to give an answer said, that nowhere was so much beauty, external and internal, to be found united, and that in the whole of Frangistan there was not a single edifice which could be compared to this.

The most familiar outward sign of the mosque is the minaret, usually a separate structure, from the roof of which the muezzin calls the believers to prayer. Mehemmed the Conqueror added a minaret to Aya Sofya; within a generation the characteristic tapering fingers pointed skyward from every quarter of the city, soaring above the crowded alleys and markets, a signal and a warning to the faithful.

The most enduring buildings erected by the Turks in Istanbul were those destined for the service of God—the mosques, medreses, and dervish cloisters on which they lavished their best materials and finest artistry. Buildings raised for human purposes—even the imperial palaces—were of more perishable materials, usually of wood, and were not infrequently destroyed, by accident or by design, and replaced by new structures. There were some buildings, for public use, which were more solidly and permanently constructed. Such for example were the covered bazaars, where the merchants had their shops and stores; the great *khans* or caravanserais—inns, warehouses, and marts at the same time, where visiting merchants could stay, keep their goods, and offer them for sale; the *hamams,* or bathhouses, of which a visitor counted 130 in Istanbul in the eighteenth century; the hospitals and asylums, hospices and almshouses, schools, colleges, and libraries.

The homes of the rich and the great were of three main types. The term *konak,* from an old Turkish word meaning a stage or halting place, was applied to town mansions, including the places of business as well as the residences of high dignitaries. The *yali* and *köshk* were both country houses, built of wood, the former a seaside villa or mansion on the shores of the Bosporus, the latter a summer retreat set amid gardens. The English word kiosk is derived from it.

In the year 1638, Evliya Efendi tells us, the Sultan Murad IV gave orders for the preparation of a comprehensive description of the city of Istanbul. The purpose was to raise help for the war against Persia:

> "In order to assist me in this great expedition, I desire that all guilds of Constantinople, both large and small, shall repair to my Imperial camp. They shall exhibit the number of their men, shops, and professions, according to their old constitutions, they shall all with their Sheikhs, Nakibs, Pirs, Agas, Kâhyas, Yigit-bashis, and Chaushes, on foot, and on horseback, with their complete eightfold music, pass before Alayköshk, that I may see how many thousand men and how many guilds there are. It shall be an Alay (procession) the like of which

never was seen before. A general description shall be made of all the Imperial mosques, of the Vizierial mosques, of the mesjids, colleges, houses for reading the Koran, and houses for reading the tradition, schools, convents, khans, baths, magazines, caravanserais, palaces of the vezirs and great men, fountains, establishments for distributing water, conduits, cisterns, quarters of Muslims, Christians, and Jews, churches and synagogues, ovens for bread and biscuits, water, wind and horse-mills, halls and repositories, of all the houses, gardens, köshks, yalis, and all the monuments to be found in the four districts, ruled by the four great Mollas of Constantinople. The inhabitants of all the quarters, the guilds, the Imams, Khatibs, and Kâhyas of the quarters shall assemble and note down every thing, and then send the complete description to my sublime Porte. Those who make the description shall be men of impartial character; if the contrary should be found I shall order them to be quartered." He gave the command that the guild of Buza-makers should pass the last of all, and no inn-keepers be found in the Imperial camp. "They shall assist the Buza-makers and serve them as *Yamak* or fellow-assistants, in the procession; they shall not be allowed to play like the other guilds their eightfold music, but pass only with cymbals and drums; it shall be known on this occasion how many Buza- and wine-houses there are, and how many inn-keepers." The Sultan issued for this purpose Hatt-i Sherifs, directed to the Grand Vizier Bayram Pasha, to the Mufti Yahya Efendi, to the Mollas of Constantinople, Eyyub, Galata, and Scutari, commanding them to make a description of all the guilds and professions with their chiefs and foundations, monuments and pious legacies. They kissed the ground, and in obeisance of the Sultan's orders they made a most complete description of the shops, guilds, foundations and monuments to be found in each quarter; it was an hundred thousand times more complete than the description, which had been made in the reign of Sultan Selim by Molla Zekeriya Efendi, because from his time till that of Sultan Murad IV Constantinople had so increased, that no room was left for any further building. The description of Constantinople and all its suburbs and villages on both sides of the Bosphorus was completed in three months. It formed a complete book, bearing the title "Description of Constantinople." The Historiographer Solakzade read it day and night in the presence of the Sultan, who exclaimed, "O my God! let this town flourish to the end of time."

According to the Imperial rescript, the following is the description of the excellent town of Constantinople. May God preserve her from decay and fall!

Under the four Mollas of Constantinople, Galata, Eyyub and Scutari, justice is transacted at six hundred and seventy tribunals. Great mosques of the Sultans, 74. Great mosques of the Viziers, 1,985. Small mosques of the town-quarters, 6,990. Other mosques great and small, 6,665. Dining establishments for the poor, 19. Hospitals, 9. Primary schools, 1,993. Houses for reading the Koran, 55. Houses for delivering the tradition, 135. Great convents, 557. Cells and rooms of Dervishes, 6,000. Sick-houses for strangers, 91. Caravansarays, 997. Khans of merchants, 565. Khans for single men, 676. Quarters of Moslims, 990. Quarters of Greeks, 354. Quarters of Jews, 657. Quarters of Franks, 17. Quarters of Armenians, 27. Palaces of Vezirs, 6,890. Baths public and private, 14,536. Fountains public and private, 9,995. Water-pipes, 989. Establishments for distributing water, 200. Fountains called Ayazma, sweet and bitter, 100. Wells, 60,000. Cisterns, 55. Magazines of water, 3,000. Covered markets, 3. Flour-halls, 37. Imperial balances, 35. Repository for grinding coffee, 2. Repository for silk, 1. Repository for wax, 1. Repository for gold-wire, 1. Repository of the custom house, 1. Repository of the land custom-house, 1. Repository for oil, 1. Repository for fish, 1. Repository for salt, 1. Repository for biscuit, 1. Repository for wine, 1. Repository for powder, 1. Repository for prisoners, 1. The Imperial Mint, 1. Magazine of cloth, 1. Magazine for corn, 1. Magazine for barley, 1. The Magazines of Bayezid, of Süleyman, of wood, of horses, of flour and of hay; of each, 1. The stables of the palace and at Vefa, 1. The Armory, 1. Prisons of State, 4. Prisons for criminals, 4. Ovens, 600. Wind-mills, 600. Water-mills, 28. Houses of the inspectors of provisions, of vegetables, of mutton, of the Inspector of the town, of the Inspector of the kitchen, of salted meat, of slaughter-houses. Barracks of the Janissaries, old and new, and of the Segbans, 162. Barracks of the Ajemioglan, the armourers, and the caulkers. The Arsenal and the barracks of the bombardiers. Four houses of Mevlevis. One house for yogurt. The paper manufactory of Battal, 1. The royal lion-house, 1. Houses for dyeing, 70. Houses for silver-ware, 10. The Musket manufactory, 1. Leaden-hall, 1. The Music-house, 1. House of the Tent-pitchers, 1. House of the Peyks, 1. House of the Painters, 1. House for the water-carriers, 1; for the gunners, 1; for the founders, 1; for the tailors, 1; for the waggoners, 1; for the fireworkers, 1; for the exercise of the Janissaries, 1; for the Samsunji, keepers of the great dogs, 1; for the Zagarji, or keepers of the pointers, 1; for the Bostanjis, 1; for the falconers, 1; for the head of the goldsmiths, 1; for the kettle-makers, 1; for the button-makers, 1; for the saddlers, 1; for the glass-makers, 1; for the head of the merchants, 2; for the vinegar-makers, 1; for the confectioners of sour fruits, 1.

I, poor Evliya . . . am now going to detail the shops, and different guilds of handicraftsmen, which exist in the town of Constantinople.

The description of the guilds of Istanbul, several hundred pages long, gives a lively and colorful picture of the rich and diversified life of the city. The guilds are divided into fifty-seven sections, and consist altogether of "a thousand and one guilds"—probably meaning no more than a very large number since only seven hundred odd are named. The first section consists of the ushers, police officers, pages, cadets (*aje-mioglans*), scavengers, sextons, sappers, pioneers, miners with hatchets, and stone-cutters.

> The Miners with hatchets, and Stonecutters . . . . They carry their implements of mining, shovels, hoes, mattocks and hatchets about them, and pass crying out "Hai" and "Hui." Their business is to level ground which would stop the march of the army, and to blow up walls.

The second section, under the general control of the police provost, contains the guilds of lictors, policemen, hangmen, thieves and footpads, press-gang men, grooms, horse-jobbers, and watchmen. Of the guilds of thieves and other immoral personages "who are innumerable," Evliya remarks that:

> They do not appear in public processions, and are not known individually, but the thieves pay tribute to the two officers of police (the Subashi and Ases-bashi) and get their subsistence by mingling in the crowds of Constantinople, and by cheating foreigners.

The proceedings of the press-gang are described in a manner reminiscent of other times and places:

> The press-gang of the Arsenal have no particular patron, and are a faithless set of people, ruled by the Kâhya of the

Arsenal. When the fleet is at Constantinople they entice poor fellows to go up with them into wine and ale-houses (Buza) putting a couple hundred piastres in their pockets: when they are drunk they chain them in the galleys under the pretext that they have spent Imperial money, and only set them free at the end of the campaign, with a pay of one thousand aspers. Sometimes they dupe them a second time by promising them two thousand aspers. They are a wonderful set of sharpers, who get quiet people into scrapes and so to the galleys.

Each section has a head, who is usually the chief of the principal guild in the section, and the guilds follow one another according to a table of precedence. Sometimes there were disputes:

The Emperor's command having been issued, that immediately after the Captains of the Mediterranean Sea the butchers were to follow, all the great Egyptian merchants of rice and hemp, of coffee, and sugar, assembled together and began to dispute with the butchers. At last they went to the Emperor's presence, where they made the following speech. "Gracious Emperor! Our ships are carrying rice, lentils, coffee, and sugar, from Egypt to Constantinople; the captains cannot do without us, and we cannot exist without them. How can these blood-shedding butchers intrude themselves between them and us! The blood-shedding of the butchers has more than once been the cause of the plague, and in order to avoid this danger their shops have been confined to a particular place outside the town. They are a set of nasty people, dealing in blood, but we afford to the capital at all times provisions of grain and vegetables." The butchers were prepared to answer, and the blood which they are wont to shed mounting into their eyes, they said: "Gracious Lord! our patron is butcher Jomerd, and our occupation and care is the sheep, an animal, which was at all times the object of God's special mercy, having been singled out as food for his servant, man. The sentence which establishes meat and flesh to be the two first of all goods is known. A poor man may subsist on a bit of flesh five or six days. It is known that we enrich the capital with our legitimate gain, whilst these merchants are a set of usurers, of whom God spoke in the Koran, saying, 'God declares sale to be lawful, but usury to be prohibited.' They bring grain and other provisions from Egypt, but accumulate them in their magazines to produce an artificial famine and to make illicit profit. The Ottomans do not want their rice of Egypt. Rice comes also from Philipopolis and Begbazari and other places. Neither do the inhabitants of Rum stand in need of Egyptian hemp, because in Rum, hemp is produced at Monastir, Kolurunia, Serfije, Tirhale, and in Anatolia at many thousand places, particularly at Trebizond, where linen and shirts are cheap and well worked, so that a Bedouin's shirt costs no more than twenty dirhems. What do we want then with their hemp, which has besides been more than once the cause of fires in Constantinople. As to lentils there is an immense quantity of them in Rum and Anatolia, and as to the Egyptian sugar, we reply, that God in the Koran has not made the eulogy of sugar but of honey, the purity of which he praises. The honey of Athens, Valentia, and Moldavia, is celebrated, each of which has seventy particular qualities, and if your Majesty should wish for sugar, many thousand quintals of it are produced at Alaya, Adalya, Adana, Selefke, Tarsus, Payas, Antakya, Aleppo, Saida, Damascus, Beirut, and Tripoli. What do we want, therefore, with Egyptian sugar, and as to the coffee it is an innovation, which curtails sleep and the generating power in man. Coffee-houses are houses of confusion. Coffee has been by law declared illicit

in the great collection of fetvas. . . . Sherbert, milk, tea, ba-
dian, salep, and almond-cream are all more wholesome than
coffee. If henna is a lawful dye for the nails of women and
beards of men, you may grind the foot of laudanum in a mor-
tar, which if transformed into a paste, dyes nails and beards of
the finest ruby-colour, kills vermin on the body and in the hair,
which it cleans from dust. There is, therefore, no necessity for
henna." The butchers having thus reviled the goods and products coming from Egypt, the Egyptian merchants replied in
the following way: "Our rice is fine and white . . . and . . .
if cooked with butter, exhales a scent like musk. It has been
produced by a wonder of the Prophet, before whose time neither rice, nor rose-water, nor bananas, no jujubes were known.
As to lentils, it is known by the tradition, that they shall grow
in paradise. Those which are watered with the water of the
Nile have more taste, and are of a larger size than the lentils
of Rumelia. It is impossible for henna to be found anywhere
better than in Egypt. The use of it is sanctified by the Sunna,
or the doings of the Prophet, and there is no reply to that.
As to sugar and hemp, we allow, that Rum stands not in need
of them, because the sugar coming from Frangistan is finer.
But say now, ye butchers! what is the profit of your trade to
the Imperial treasury? we give of the cargoes of our fleet coming from Egypt annually no less than eleven thousand purses
to the customs. If your Majesty adverts to our just claims, our
precedency over the butchers in public entrances must be decided in our favour." The merchants having ended their speech,
the Mufti Yahya Efendi and Muid Ahmed Efendi read the
passage of the tradition: "The best of men is he who is useful
to mankind," meantime the Emperor made out an Imperial
rescript, by which the precedence of the merchants over the
butchers was decided, to the great delight of the first, who,

leaping for joy, passed immediately after the captains of the Mediterranean.

Once a year the guilds held a public procession:

This procession of the Imperial camp begins its march at dawn, and continues the whole day till sunset. It is opened by the Chaushes called Alay-chaush, and amounts to the number of two hundred thousand men, all passing armed like a thundering sea. It is an established custom, that each of these guilds, when arrived near the new garden, at the monument of Hosrev-pasha, present themselves before the house of the judge of Constantinople, because he is the authority, which has the inspection of all measures and weights, and assembles the guilds. It is the law that all these guilds should present the Molla or Judge of Constantinople with the wares and merchandises, which they had exposed in the public show; but some are abstracted on this occasion. After this respect is paid to the first magistrate of the capital, the guilds accompany their officers to their lodgings, and every one returns home. All trade and worksmanship is interrupted at Constantinople, on account of this procession, for a period of three days, during which the riot and confusion of the procession fills the town to a degree, which is not to be expressed by language, and which only I, poor Evliya, dared to give an idea of. No where else has such a procession been seen, or shall be seen. . . . Such is the crowd and population of that great capital Constantinople which may God guard from all celestial and earthly mischief, and let her be inhabited till the end of the world.

A few of the guilds may be cited as examples:

The Merchants of salted beef are six hundred . . . wealthy merchants . . . . The greatest part of them are infidels of Moldavia and Wallachia. . . . They bring, about the day of Kassem [S. Demetrius], three hundred thousand oxen for the provision of Constantinople, of which they made Pasdirma [salted beef]. They sell their cattle outside the Seven Towers, where they keep it in the ditch. The excise is paid to the Inspector of salted beef, and the quarrels are decided by the Naib of salted beef. It is a large beef-market, lasting forty days. In the official statement given to Murad IV, it is related that in the time when Ali Aga was inspector of the Customhouse, and Hüseyn the Naib of salted beef, three hundred thousand bulls were immolated. The patron of these drivers of sheep and cattle is not known. The heads and feet of the victims are dressed by the cooks. These sheep and cattle driving merchants pass on Arabian horses, well dressed, and are a wonderfully clean troop. . . .

The Sherbet-merchants are five hundred men, with three hundred shops. They ornament their shops with many thousand cups and bowls of china and fayence, which are filled with sherbet, made of rhubarb, roses, lemons, lotus, tamarinds, and grapes. They pass presenting these sherbets to the spectators. The most famous of all the sherbet-shops is that of the Bedouin sherbet-merchant, opposite the monument of Tay Zade . . . near the fountain of Mahmud Pasha. In Arabia, Persia, and Turkey, there is no sherbet-merchant to be compared to him. People crowd into his shop, where he prepares sherbet for the viziers and the first men of the Empire. . . .

The Snow and Ice merchants have an establishment near the vegetable-market, where the chief of the Imperial ice-porters resides summer and winter. Three hundred boatmen under his direction are always on excursions to the mountains of Katirli, Mudanya, and Olympus. They embark the snow, ice, and fresh water, from these mountains, and carry them to the Imperial kitchen, to the confectionary, to the Harem, and to the houses of the grand vizier and other great men. The porters who carry the ice and snow from the mountains down to the sea are the muleteers of Mudanya, the wandering tribes of Bursa and stone cutters. The chief of the ice-men has the inspection of nine magazines established in the neighbourhood of Constantinople. . . . In the winter, when it snows, the grand vizier, the Aga of the Janissaries, the Bostanjibashi, the Kapudan-Pasha, with a crowd of two hundred thousand men, carrying shovels, assemble at the Ok-maydan, and heaping up the snow in large masses throw it into the snow magazines. . . .

The Fishermen, who fish with the nets called Karatia. We have counted in the harbour of Constantinople, from the Seraglio Point to Eyyub, on both sides of the shore, an hundred and fifty nets called Karatia. Ten fishermen, descended from the Greeks who opened the gate of Petri to Mehemmed II, are even now free of all kinds of duties, and give no tithe to the Inspector of fisheries. Karatia is the name of the fishing apparatus, which consists of a yard or pole stretching out from a house on the shore, with a square net fastened to the end of it, by which the fish are caught. The Greeks inhabiting the shore of the harbour are all subject to the jurisdiction of the Bostanjibashi, without whose leave they are not allowed to fix a stake in the sea; they pay to him for every stake a ducat. The fishermen who are free of duty, are obliged to hunt dolphins, which serve as medicine for the Emperor. They know the places where they hide themselves amongst the Prince's Islands; if any one else were to chase them, he would be punished. . . .

The Slave-merchants are two thousand men, they use the rooms of the great Khan, where the slave-market is established. These people dress in the finest array, on the day of the public procession, the slaves from Circassia, Mingrelia, Dadian, &c. which they have bought, as legal booty, and pass them in review before the Emperor at the Imperial Köshk. The Emperor then takes an hundred brilliant Georgians, Abaza, and Circassians, for the Imperial Saray, rewarding their owners with magnificent presents. The train is closed by the Inspector of the slaves, before whom walk many hundred fine girls, set off by most costly apparel. They are followed by some thousand fine boys, with radiant eyes and faces, who, instead of . . . pages, walk before and around the inspector. . . .

The Stamp-men. The Stamp-office is a great building close to the factory of the goldsmiths, with a garden and bath, wherein seventy men are employed. They stamp the Tughra [Imperial cypher] on all the silver worked at Constantinople, which however differs from the Tughra on the coins, in as much as the words "ever victorious" are on it. The chief of the stamp-office is at the same time the inspector of all the goldsmiths, because he puts the stamp on their work after having made the assay of the silver. The tax for the stamp is six aspers, three of which go to the treasury and three are divided between the head of the stamp-office and the three Sufis of the tower; if the three Sufis dare to stamp silver of lower alloy than is prescribed, their heads are cut off and righteous men appointed in their places. If the silver put in the fire for the assay is found to be impure, the chief of the stamp-office confiscates it for the Emperor, or breaks it with a hammer into small pieces and gives it back to the owner; he does the same with silver buttons, if found to be hollow, or to be filled with some spurious alloy. All this is according to the *ḳanun* of Sultan Selim I, who was himself at the same time a goldsmith, dye-cutter and stamper. The building devoted to the stampoffice is his foundation.

The Tailors. They have two great establishments, the first close to the menagerie of lions, built by Mehemmed II, which is the house where the chief resides; the second opposite the Alayköshk, built by Sultan Süleyman; at each of them five hundred men are working. The number of the tailors' shops outside of Constantinople amounts to three thousand in all the quarters of the four jurisdictions of the capital, and the number of men are five thousand. . . . Besides the two chiefs of the Imperial tailors, who reside at the aforesaid two establishments, there is a third, who is the chief of all tailors both in and out of the town. They ornament their shops on litters, with all kinds of precious dresses, and carry on poles a great number of clothes made of Egyptian stuffs, and their boys are all clad in armour, because they are a most necessary guild in the camp, and have, therefore, obtained rank before the following corporations. . . .

The Tanners. There are twelve good tanneries in the four jurisdictions of Constantinople. These tanners are a set of wild fellows, and men-dragons; who, if a criminal, or blood-stained villain takes refuge amongst them, refuse to deliver him up to justice, but they do not let him escape, but put him to the business of turning up dog's dirt, an occupation which causes him to repent of former crimes and to amend his life afterwards. There are altogether seven hundred tanneries, which employ three thousand men. . . . These tanners are a wild and savage set of men and were the cause of the late Malek Ahmed Pasha losing the place of grand vizier; they are so riotous and unruly, that if assembled together they would be capable of deposing the Emperor. At the public entrance to the camp, many thousand of them assembled barefoot and bareheaded, with hands and feet coloured red, and with arms and nails of a deep blue or black, all dressed in leather and saffian of variegated colours, their aprons, turbans, dolmans, and clubs being made of leather, crying "Astra, Astra." Others are busy adorning their shops with saffian of different colours, blue, yellow, peach-coloured, Nafta; others pass turning goat-skins in wooden vessels, and treading them, with cries of "Ya-Hai!" (O, all vivifying) Others pass saying: "We clean what is unclean, what is unclean, we clean." . . .

The Shoemakers are four thousand men, with three hundred and forty shops. They have seven factories in the Coral market, where no less than eight thousand single men all employed in this guild are lodged. They have their particular officers, who are appointed by an Imperial Rescript of Sultan Süleyman, who exempted them from the jurisdiction of all other commanding officers. They punish their culprits themselves, even by death, and bury them in the precincts of their establishment. Sultan Süleyman once swore in his wrath against the Janissaries, who being dissatisfied would not touch their soup, that he would break them with the assistance of the shoemakers, who having heard of his oath, assembled instantly from the four jurisdictions of Constantinople; an armed crowd of forty thousand shoemakers, who made their appearance before the palace with shouts of "Allah, Allah." Süleyman, surprised by these cries, asked their cause, and pleased with their faithfulness, he gave audience to the chiefs and seniors, asking what he could do for them in reward for their zeal. Their petition embraced four points. First, they said that formerly boy-recruits had been given to them, who, well-bred and taught to read and write, could make their way to military charges, but as this custom had been suspended by the Janissaries, they begged its renewal. Secondly, they lamented that the price of ten aspers was too low for a pair of papushes, and wished it encreased. In the third place, they petitioned for the free execution of their culprits by their own officers, without any other magistrate's interference. In the fourth place, they begged to be granted the privilege of a particular train with Turkish music, at the public processions, because till then their Aga had been confounded in the train of the Aga of the boy-recruits. Süleyman granted them these four points by an Imperial diploma, and bade them go home, and be quiet and keep ready as before. The Janissaries, who before had no mind to eat their soup, grew now of so good an appetite, that they were nearly devouring the plates together with the soup. The shoemakers pass all armed, but barefoot and bareheaded, adorning their shops with all kinds of shoes and slippers, of all possible dimensions. . . .

The Arak-makers are three hundred men, with one hundred shops. . . . They extract spirits from all kinds of plants. . . . It is sin to get intoxicated with these kinds of Araks, but to taste one or two drops is not illegal.

From the Black Sea and the Mediterranean, from the Danube and the Nile, merchants and government agents supplied the immense daily needs of the city population in bread, meat, and other foodstuffs. Importers and manufacturers brought them clothes, adornments, and luxuries. Money flowed into the city from the taxes and tribute of the provinces, the income of fiefs, grants, estates, and offices, and the profits of trade. There were rich men in the city, living in splendid houses. Besides the many whose wealth derived from the exercise of power or the holding of office, there were prosperous merchants and financiers, men of far-reaching enterprises.

The guilds, and especially the brotherhoods of merchants and artisans, played an important role in the social and corporate life of the city, corresponding tò certain aspects of the civic and public life of the cities of Greco-Roman antiquity and of the West. Ottoman Istanbul, like other Islamic cities, had no real corporate civic identity, no communal or municipal institutions. Medieval Islam was essentially an urban civilization, and reached its highest points of achievement in a series of brilliant and flourishing cities; yet Islamic law and Islamic government never really recognized the city as such. Classical Islamic legal theory does not admit corporate persons, and allows little place for representative institutions; Islamic history shows no publicly recognized, legally privileged cities, with corporate identity and status, and well-defined limits and rights, like those of Europe. Without citizenship and without civic institutions, the city was governed by two groups of men. The first consisted of officers of the sovereign, both civil and military, exercising a delegated and revocable authority deriving from the sovereign power; their principal concern was with police duties, fire fighting, and public security generally. The second group were men of religion, members of the ulema class, entrusted with certain duties of prevention, adjudication, and enforcement, where the provisions of the Islamic law were concerned.

The Ottoman city of Istanbul was divided for administrative purposes into four units—Istanbul proper, and the "three towns" of Galata, Eyyub, and Üsküdar (Scutari). Istanbul was the ancient triangular-shaped city of Constantinople built on a group of hills bounded by the Golden Horn, the Sea of Marmara, and the great land-walls that stretched from sea to sea. At the base of the triangle, starting from Seraglio Point, was the Topkapi Palace, with its vast grounds and its manifold buildings and departments. Beyond the Imperial Gate in its outer perimeter lay the great Hippodrome square, with Aya Sofya. From there the road led to the summit of the third hill, the old center of the city, with the Old Palace of Mehemmed the Conqueror, the mosque of Bayezid, and, not far away, the entrance to the great bazaar and the mosque complex of Süleyman the Magnificent.

On the opposite shore of the Golden Horn lay the suburb of Galata. In Byzantine times it had been a colony of European, especially Genoese merchants. It remained so under the Turks until modern times, with a population predominantly non-Muslim and non-Turkish. Some Muslims were however established there, and two institutions were of particular importance—the Galata Saray school, part of the palace educational system, and the convent of the Mevlevi (Dancing) dervishes founded there in 1492, the oldest Mevlevi establishment in the capital. The hills north of Galata became a favorite place of residence for foreign envoys and consuls; there too lived the famous Luigi Gritti, an illegitimate son of the Doge of Venice, who became adviser and confidante to the Grand Vizier Ibrahim Pasha, in the days of Süleyman the Magnificent. The Turks called him *Bey-oglu* — the prince's son—and in time gave this name to the whole of Galata and its extensions. The Europeans called it Pera, from a Greek word meaning beyond or across—i.e., across the Golden Horn from old Istanbul.

At the northern end of the Golden Horn, beyond the walls of the city, was the suburb of Eyyub, named after an ancient Arab companion and flag-bearer of the Prophet, who is said to have fallen during the first Arab attempt to seize the city from the Byzantines in 672. Mehemmed the Conqueror built a mosque and tomb there, and the prestige of this sanctuary

became so great, that the enthronement ceremony of the Ottoman Sultans, the girding of the sword, was performed in it.

The suburb of Üsküdar lay across the straits on the Asian
shore, facing the old city of Istanbul. This had been in Turkish possession for at least a century at the time of the fall of
Constantinople, and was already to a large extent Turkish
and Islamic. After 1453 it became in effect a part of the capital
though, according to Evliya, it did not really develop until
the time of Süleyman the Magnificent. It became an important religious center, with many famous mosques and medreses; it was, in particular, the seat of a number of dervish
convents, notably one of the Rifai or Howling dervishes. Galata, Eyyub, and Üsküdar were together known as *bilad-i
selase,* the three towns.

The maintenance of order in the capital was entrusted to
certain officers of the armed forces; it was carried out through
a system of day and night patrols operating from a network
of guardhouses in and about the city. The Bostanji-bashi,
commandant of the Palace gardeners, a distinguished regi-
ment of the imperial household, was responsible for the po-
licing of the ports and shores of the Golden Horn, the Bosporus, and the Sea of Marmara. It was his practice to patrol
the coasts and waterways in a boat, with an escort of thirty
men. The Kapudan-Pasha, the admiral of the fleet, was in
charge of the commercial port and district of Galata and of
the naval base and arsenal at Kasim Pasha, and policed them
with patrols of sailors led by naval officers. The commandants of the corps of gunners and armorers (*topju-bashi* and
jebeji-bashi) had similar duties in the areas adjoining their
bases and depots. Elsewhere in the city the aga of the Janis-

saries was generally responsible for public order and security. A number of senior Janissary officers, under his command, were especially concerned with police matters. Their duties were to police the streets, to prevent and punish crime, and to execute the decisions and sentences of the religious authorities, whom they upheld in their function of administering and enforcing the laws of Islam and the rulings of the Sultan.

Each of the "three towns" had its own *ƙadi,* or judge, independent of the *ƙadi* of Istanbul, though of lower rank in the religious hierarchy. The four *ƙadis* were responsible for judicial and religious matters in the metropolitan area, and together attended on the grand vizier every Wednesday. Another member of the ulema class, with important duties in the city, was the *muhtesib,* whose responsibility it was to enforce the laws and regulations relating to the prices and quality of goods offered for sale in the markets, and in general to maintain standards of public decency and morality.

Some idea of the problems with which the religious authorities had to deal may be gained from an order dated 23 Rebi ül-Evvel 981 (July 23, 1573) sent from the Imperial Divan to the *Kadi* of Istanbul.

> Order to the Kadi of Istanbul. In former times the infidels were forbidden to bring wine into the cities, and the collection of taxes from wine was foregone. The infidels, however, have by trickery brought in wine after all, and since no tax was collected the treasury suffered serious loss. This matter was referred to the chief Mufti, the most learned of the ulema of the time, who rules as follows: "It is lawful to collect the tithe at the half-rate on wine brought by non-Muslim subjects of the Sultan, and at the full rate on wine brought by foreign

infidels. It is, however, certainly not lawful publicly to import wine into cities where the Friday prayer is performed, nor is it lawful for them to sell publicly to one another the wine which they have bought secretly, still less to sell it to Muslims. When they sell wine to one another let them in no way make this public."

Acting in accordance with this noble fetva, a commissioner has been appointed to collect the tithe on wine, and an Imperial order to this effect has been issued. At the present time it has been made known to me that Jews and Christians in the God-guarded city of Istanbul, contrary to the noble fetva and to my Imperial order, are publicly introducing wine and spirits in barrels, casks, and skins, and are holding feasts and playing music at their gatherings and parties. I have therefore decreed that, as soon as this order reaches you, you shall give clear and proper warning to the Jews and Christians, and also to the *Kapijis* of the God-guarded city, not to bring wine and spirits publicly into the city in barrels, casks or skins, not to sell to Muslims that which they bring secretly by night for their own use, and to keep their sales of wines among themselves secret; not to turn their houses into taverns, or sell wines and spirits publicly; not to perform music at their feasts. . . .

Another aspect of the work of the Islamic authorities is shown in an order, dated 26 Ramazan 993 (September 21, 1585), rejecting an application from the butchers of Istanbul for a remission of taxes:

Order to the Kadi of Istanbul. You have stated in a letter to us that the butchers of the God-guarded city have come to the court of the Holy Law, saying: "While the authorized price of mutton in the God-guarded city is one Oke [400 dirhams] for 3 aspers, in accordance with an old *kanun* it must be sold to

Janissaries at the rate of 150 dirhams for 1 asper. In 5½ months of the year 993, we have slaughtered 23,500 head of sheep and sold them to Janissaries at the prescribed price. Because of the resulting losses which we have suffered, we are now unable to pay the debt of 200,000 aspers which we owe to the cattle-dealers." You have further stated that when they asked for a gracious remission of the butcher's tax due from them, Ilyas Chaush, the sheep commissioner, confirmed the truth of what they said.

In this matter my decree has been issued that the law must be observed. I have commanded that . . . whatever the ancient law may be, you must act in accordance with it and henceforth avoid anything contrary to it. . . .

Food and drink held an important place among the pre-occupations of the religious and police authorities in the city. So too for a while did coffee and tobacco, the former intro-duced from the Arab lands, the latter by English merchants from the American colonies. The historian Ibrahim-i Pechevi, writing in about 1635, describes their introduction as follows:

Until the year 962 [1555], in the high, God-guarded capital city of Constantinople, as well as in the Ottoman lands gen-erally, coffee and coffee-houses did not exist. About that year, a fellow called Hakam from Aleppo, and a wag called Shems from Damascus came to the city; they each opened a large shop in the district called Tahtalkale, and began to purvey coffee. These shops became meeting-places of a circle of pleasure-seekers and idlers, and also of some wits from among the men of letters and literati, and they used to meet in groups of about twenty or thirty. Some read books and fine writings, some were busy with backgammon and chess, some brought new poems and talked of literature. Those who used to spend a good deal of money on giving dinners for the sake of convivial entertainment, found that they could attain the joys of conviviality merely by spending an asper or two on the price of coffee. It reached such a point that all kinds of unemployed officers, judges and professors all seeking preferment, and corner-sitters with nothing to do proclaimed that there was no place like it for pleasure and relaxation, and filled it until there was no room to sit or stand. It became so famous that, besides the holders of high offices, even great men could not refrain from coming there. The Imams and muezzins and pious hypocrites said: "People have become addicts of the coffee house; nobody comes to the mosques!" The ulema said: "It is a house of evil deeds; it is better to go to the wine-tavern than there." The preachers in particular made great efforts to forbid it. The muftis, arguing that anything which is heated to the point of carbonization, that is, becomes charcoal, is unlawful, issued fetvas against it. In the time of Sultan Murad III, may God pardon him and have mercy on him, there were great interdictions and prohibitions, but certain persons made approaches to the chief of police and the captain of the watch about selling coffee from back-doors in side-alleys, in small and unobtrusive shops, and were allowed to do this. . . . After this time, it became so prevalent, that the ban was abandoned. The preachers and muftis now said that it does not get completely carbonized, and to drink it is therefore lawful. Among the ulema, the sheykhs, the viziers and the great, there was nobody left who did not drink it. It even reached such a point that the grand viziers built great coffee houses as investments, and began to rent them out at one or two gold pieces a day.

On the coming of "the fetid and nauseating smoke of tobacco" he says:

The English infidels brought it in the year 1009 [A.D. 1600–1601], and sold it as a remedy for certain diseases of humidity. Some companions from among the pleasure-seekers and sensualists said: "Here is an occasion for pleasure" and they became addicted. Soon those who were not mere pleasure-seekers also began to use it. Many even of the great ulema and the mighty fell into this addiction. From the ceaseless smoking of the coffee-house riff-raff the coffee-houses were filled with blue smoke, to such a point that those who were in them could not see one another. In the markets and bazaars too their pipes never left their hands. Puff-puffing in each other's faces and eyes, they made the streets and markets stink. In its honour they composed silly verses, and declaimed them without occasion.

Sometimes I had arguments with friends about it. I said: "Its abominable smell taints a man's beard and turban, the garment on his back and the room where it is used; sometimes it sets fire to carpets and felts and bedding, and soils them from end to end with ash and cinders; after sleep its evil vapour rises to the brain; and, not content with this, its ceaseless use withholds men from toil and gain and keeps hands from work. In view of this and other similar harmful and abominable effects, what pleasure or profit can there be in it?"

To this the only answer they could give was: "It is an amusement, and moreover a pleasure of aesthetic taste." But there is no possibility of spiritual pleasure from this, which could pertain to matters of aesthetic taste. This answer is no answer. It is pure pretension.

Apart from all this, it has several times been the cause of great fires in the high God-guarded city of Constantinople. Several hundred thousand people suffered from those fires. Only this much is conceded, that it is of use for the guarding of galley-slaves, as the guards on the ships can to some extent ward off sleep by using it, and that, by guarding against humidity, it induces dryness. But it is not permissible, according to reason or tradition, to perpetuate such great damage for such small benefit. By the beginning of the year 1045 [A.D. 1635–36], its spread and fame were such that they could not be written or expressed.

In spite of these repressions, there were soon many of these places, dispensing coffee, tobacco, and good conversation, and attracting the wits and literati, scholars and officials of the city. Shems is said to have returned to Aleppo, after only three years, with a profit of five thousand gold pieces. Bostanzade Mehmed Efendi, chief mufti from 1589 to 1592 and from 1593 to 1598, even delivered a detailed *fetva,* in verse, giving his approval of this drink which an Arab poet had called "The negro enemy of sleep and love." Other, more conservative ulema were hostile, and the discussion of public affairs in these places seems to have caused some alarm to the authorities, who issued decrees against them—with little effect. In 1633, Murad IV, well known for his severity, prohibited both coffee and tobacco, and executed a number of coffee-drinkers and smokers. The stated reason was to protect the city from fire; another purpose may have been to safeguard the government from comment. Pechevi approved wholeheartedly:

May Almighty God add increase to the life and might and justice and equity of our sovereign emperor (God strengthen his helpers), who has closed all the coffee houses throughout the divinely guarded realms and caused suitable shops to be opened in their place, and who has commanded that smoking be totally forbidden. By this means he has conferred such great boons and benefactions on the rich and poor alike, that if they thank him until the Day of Judgment, they will not properly discharge their debt of gratitude.

After some further arguments and reversals, the "tasteless," as the opponents of coffee and tobacco were called, accepted defeat. Tobacco was finally declared licit in a *fetva* of the Chief Mufti Mehmed Baha'i Efendi, himself a heavy smoker who had been dismissed and exiled for smoking in 1634. His contemporary Kâtib Chelebi says of him, however, that his ruling in favor of tobacco was prompted, not by his own addiction, but by a concern for what was best suited to the condition of the people, and a belief in the legal principle that all that is not explicitly forbidden is permitted.

The coffee houses were not the only distraction of the citizens of Istanbul. A favorite pastime was the picnic, and there were many well-loved picnic grounds in the environs of the city, to which the court and the people used to resort in the summer and autumn. Especially popular were the little fresh-water streams, with woods and gardens on their banks, to which picnic parties came from Istanbul, rowed in gaily decked caiques, to disport themselves and converse amid the trees, the fountains, and the flowers. Such was the "Little River," Küçüksu, on the Asian shore of the Bosporus, which Europeans called "the Sweet Waters of Asia"; such too was Kâthane, at the upper end of the Golden Horn, known to visitors as "the Sweet Waters of Europe." Kâthane, which took its name from an old Byzantine paper mill, had been a favorite picnic resort since the days of the conquest, and had been beautified by Süleyman the Magnificent and other Sultans. In 1721, Ahmed III built there the famous Summer Palace of Sa'dabad, "the place of felicity," based on plans of a French château brought by his ambassador in Paris, with avenues of trees, gardens and pavilions, fountains, jets, and waterfalls, and multitudes of variegated tulips, then at the height of fashion.

Some entertainments were provided by the Sultan—public festivities, with sporting contests, displays, fireworks and illuminations, to celebrate victories, religious holidays, and other festive occasions. One such festival was held in honor of the circumcision of Prince Mehemmed, son of Sultan Murad III, in 1582 during the war against Persia. It was described in detail by a European visitor, who had his own—not untraditional—explanation of the purpose of these entertainments. An English version appeared in London a couple of years later.

> In the yeere of our Lord and Saviour, 1582, the Soldan Amurathe, Emperor of Turkie, seeing his affayres to be in evyll order, perceyving also the contrarietie of affections in his Subiectes dyd now determine with himselfe to winne the good will, and to be better beloved, and more esteemed of his then before, and also to be more redouted, and had in greater estimation amongst Straungers, and forreine Nations and Countries then ever, thought it necessarie and very requisute to make a great solemnitie in the Circumcising of Soldan Mahumet his Sonne: and for the better performing of his purposed determination, dyd summon together the greatest part of all Christian Princes, to the end that this Feast might be solemnized, as it were before the eyes of the whole world: And in deede, the Ambassadours of many Christian Princes, and Mahumets, were

sent unto Constantinople that is to saye, the Ambassadour of the Emperor of Fraunce, of Polognie, of Venice, of Persia, of Fees [Morocco] and of Tartaria, of Transilvania, and of Moldavia, with many other Princes. . . .

Now to declare unto you, the place wherein sundrie sortes of Playes and Pastimes were showne, it was mervailous great and large, wherein was created great Theaters and Scaffolds of woodde, distinguished and separated into diverse parts, as if they were Chambers appointed for everie Ambassador, places as well to banquet in, as also for to beholde the Plaies and Pastimes. Amurathe, was in the most fayre and ritchest place of all the rest, from whence he might through lattisses, or grates, see everie one, without being seene of any one. Behinde him was his Mother, his Wife and his Sister: and on the one side of him was Sinan Bassa, his Lieuetenant generall, then the rest of his Carles and noble men, on the other side was the Ambassadors of the aforesayde Kings and Princes. In the middest of all these Theaters there was a fayre Tyltyard, all open and discovered, eighteen hundred paces long, and twelve hundred paces broade, verie finelie paved: and in the same there was two most excellent and auncient Pyramidesses, the one of marble fowre square, verie cunninglie made, and the foote of it to upholde this Pyramides, there was fowre great and mighty pillers, fowre square, and round at the toppe. . . . the other was of stone cunningly erected, without any kinde of simonde or morter . . . and neere unto these Pyramides, there were certaine peeces of woodde, set up verie high, so that they did appeare much more higher then the Pyramides, these peeces of wood had betwixt them reaching from the one to the other, engines made of corde, composed in the manner of a Tabernacle, to the which was tyed an infinite number of Lampes, verie splendisaunt, moste dexteriouslie handled, which cast a great lyght throughout all the place. There was also a wheele, much like unto Myll wheele, the which turned continuallie of it selfe. There were also five Images, in fourme and fashion lyke unto great pyllers, verie high made, all of Waxe, and paynted with divers collours, verie splendisaunt, and shyning brightlie, because of the golde wherewithall they were garnished: to be short, all things were verie methodically and sumptuously set foorth.

Nowe the daye of Circumcision approching, which was the eighteene of Maie, in the yeere aforesayde, Amurath and his Sonne accompaned with Dukes and Carles, and many other Officers, together with many thousands of people martched foorth, with great tryumph out of his Castle, dyrectlie unto the place appointed, for these Playes and pastimes: and as they discended from horseback, there was showne unto them in the base Court of the Castle, three hundred straunge Beastes, made all of Sugar, verie diverselie disposed and ingeniously invented. That doone, the Sonne of Amurathe followed with great and more braver troops of men then before, went towardes his Mother: for it is the custome of the Turkes, in the Cyrcumcizing of the Sonne of theyre Soldan or Seigniour, that this Sonne before his Cyrcumcizion, must goe and give the Dirnear adieu, and last farewell unto his Mother, whoe he seeth no more: after that, he being now arrived at his Mothers Pallace leaving all his trayne apart, he went unto her reverently dooing his duetie, remayned with her alone the space of two howres: after long conference he humbly tooke his leave and departed from her, dyrectly unto the place of pastimes, the manner whereof, I wyll declare unto you, as heereafter followeth. . . .

Now followeth it, to speake of the playes, sports, and pastimes, the which I wil declare unto you in three articles, how they were represented, & shewed at three sundry times. The one sort whereof were called forenoone sports: another were called afternoone sports: and then the last of all midnight sportes. The inhabitants, and Artificers of Constantinople . . . those forenoone sports with all theyr royall and brave attyre. The souldiors and men of warr, the labourers, the minstrels, the leapers, and dauncers, the juglers, and suchlyke, did employ and busie themselves about the forenoone sports. The midnight sports were passed away with burning of Fortresses, Holdes, Horsses, Elephantes, and other creatures made by arte. . . . .

I must now set downe for the afterward, and last company, the Singers, Players of Instruments, Schollers, Monkes, Juglers, Tumblers, and Plaiers: people which among the Turkes are as like them in fashion of living, in apparell, & in styrring from place to place, as one drop of milke is like unto another, neither better nor worsser: the heart of the singers and Musicians, had great good agreement and concorde, with the armie of seditious souldiors: there you might have seen Arabians, Mores, Persians, Grecians, and Spaniardes, sounding of theyr Cornets, Trumpets, Tabors, Cyterons, and other Instrumentes within the Parke, or Tiltyard, where they made such a confused noyse and sound, without tune, change of note, or keeping of tune and space, that all the whole Toune sounded and rong with the route of theyr voices, and soundes. Last of all, marched on the Scholers, which of a truth you would not have judged to have been such: but rather you would have taken them for Pilgrimes, and begging Friers: for a man could not have presumed any otherwise of them, seeing them wrapped in such coverings, with white hattes tyed about the myddle with stringes: bare-footed, with fowle dyrtie handes, and a most filthy and yrksome countenance to beholde: they presented unto Amurathe certaine bookes, and painted papers of theyr owne invention. The Monkes followed after them, with a company of poore pilgrimes, which goe in pilgimage to Mecque, as they call it, which is the Sepulchre of Mahomet, they are counted verie holie men in Turkie: cloathed lyke Scholers, which doo nothing but labour and trotte up and downe with theyr bodies, making themselves leane, as in the ende, they loose all theyr witte and understanding: and because they rested, nor stayed not in any one place at any time, but always were skipping, and dauncing about: a man might verie well compare them unto Curetes, and Corybantes, the aun-cient Priests of Cybele, the graund mother of the two Paganes: unto them it was among all other, that Amurathe cause many small presentes to be made. They were presentlie followed by Players, more in number then flies or gnattes, one sort mask-ing wise, other some having Myters, like Popes, and crowns: balde, and half shaven, theyr visages of all most straunge: with Goates beardes, theyr mouthes wide open, as if they would have swallowed up as many as looked uppon them: some of them having theyr garmentes all to broken, and as it were fieade over theyr eares: other some halfe naked, and halfe covered, and other some altogether naked and shameless without meas-ure. . . .

But I will first beginne with the Combat of the Wrastlers, an exercise very much sette by among the Auncients, and such a one, as did verye much delight as many as behelde the same: For the Herauld had no sooner ended his proclamation, and crye, but straight wayes came foorth in to the same place xv. couple of wrastlers, all naked and oyled after the olde fashion, to catch holde the one by the other, every one by his com-panion: one amongst the rest, pricked and praunced on, and sette out himselfe in the middest of the place, showing his broad shoulders, shaking his armes, and as Dares did, whereof Virgil maketh mention, challenge and provoking the reste to wrastle: and suddainly a young man came in before him, which was to fight, no lesse stronge, nor stoute then the other, and he beganne lustilie to cast uppe his legges, and his fistes into the ayre, then having made a prayer with a loude voyce, and marching a little up and downe, to make himself somewhat nimble and plyant, hee layes me fast holde upon him, as had so defyed him, by and by they came unto handy gripes, and to graple themselves together, laying eache upon the grounde, flatt upon their noses, then rysing uppe againe, they fell to it lustily, sometimes thrusting and pushing, and sometime clyping, and colling eache other very straightlie: sometime shifting of places, and lifting one another aloft into the ayre. The one of them went about to catch the other fast by the legge, whereby he should leese his offered blowes and breath and all together, but he therewith unfolded and untwined his legges, and setteth upon the other as earnestlie, for to make him loose all that laboure: nowe they having beene at their prises for the space of three howres, they were bothe so weary, so soultry whot, and so out of breath, and yet so fleshed one against an other, with choller, and shame to see the whole Courte standing, and watching all ye while upon them, giving iudgment on them, so that in the Ende, they were well faine to give over and rest themselves, and then Amurath commanded them to depart. Then came the other also in their order, but they wrestled not so stoutly, nor yet so long as the first did. And this is al that the wrastlers did. . . .

Let us nowe then conclude, (if it please you) and let us describe unto you, the sightes which they made, and were to be seene in the night: and although that they were not much unlyke unto the day sportes yet I will in breefe declare them unto you. Presentlie and immediatelie after sunne set, they lighted their Lampes which were hanged up in the Tabernacle, and in the wheels made of cordes: (whereof I have spoken heretofore) the which Lampes turned verie round by art & cunning, and burned verie cleare, and lyght all the whole night. Moreover, there were every night, lighted in the sayd Parke, to the number of thyrtie Lynks, or Torches, from the which, all the whole Theatre, received a most famous and cleare lyght, and brightnesse. Now these thinges being in this order disposed, they shotte off squibbes full of powder, which made a marvailous noyse and sounde: and as they fell upon the ground, they spette out six or seven sparkles, lyke unto starres, and verie pleasaunt to beholde.

Then after all this, they brought in everie day, day by day into this Cloister six, eight, and at the most, ten Fortresses, Towers, or shippes, made of boords, covered properlie with paper, or with fine linnen cloath, gylded, and verie ritch, and sumptuous made, with diverse paintings and collours, and then they gave fyre unto them: they were made strong, both within and without, and of all sides, with short pieces, lyke unto Mortiers, which are a kinde of Artillerie of yron, short, and having many ringes or cyrcles, onely used in shippes for nayle shotte, being well appointed, with squibbs, and with powder for the Cannons, without any lacke or want thereof. And as soone as they put too fyre, there presentlie followes a noyse lyke lyghtning and straunge thunder. These squibbes dyd flee about in the likenesse of Serpentes, and were powred out round about the Theatre: and to make an ende of this brute or noyse, they had in theyr company, the sounds of Trumpettes and Tabors. These so fearefull noyses were nothing at all pleasaunt, but rather shewed, and betokened the assault, and taking of *Constantinople.* Furthermore, you should have seene the shapes, and figures of men, cloathed after the Persian, Italian, and Allemaigne fashion: also the shapes and figures of Elephantes, Camelles, Dogges, Horsses, Asses, Wildefowle, and other lyke creatures, all full of Cannon shotte and powder, unto the which they put fyre, and then they were all brought to nothing.

These sportes lasted and continued, untyll two of the clocke, and sometime (at the commaundement of Amurath) until three of the clocke after midnight. . . .

VI. Faith and Learning

AMONG THE CHRISTIAN PEOPLES of Europe it was the common practice, at one time, to use the word Turk as a synonym of Muslim, and to speak of a convert to Islam, of whatever nationality, as having "turned Turk." This usage was not without good reasons. The Ottoman Empire from its foundation to its end was an Islamic state, dedicated first to the advancement, then to the defense of Islam against the infidels. From the sixteenth century its territories included the old heartlands of Islam—the holy cities of Mecca and Medina, the capitals of the ancient caliphs in Damascus and Baghdad. This was the last, perhaps the greatest, certainly the most enduring of the great universal Islamic empires. In the parlance of its writers and officials, its sovereign was the sovereign of Islam, its armies were the armies of Islam, its laws were the laws of Islam, which it was the sultan's duty to uphold and administer. In this task, he was assisted by a great hierarchy of scholars and divines, the custodians of the Holy Law.

It has often been said that there is no priesthood in Islam—that is to say, there is no sacerdotal office, no priestly mediation between man and God. It might also be said that there are no lawyers in Islam, in the sense that Islam recognizes no human legislative function, and no valid system of law other than the law of God. In fact, however, there grew up from early times a class of professional men of religion who fulfilled the task of both lawyers and priests—the doctors of the Holy Law, the jurist-divines of Islam. In Islam there is no clear division between law and religion, nor between crime and sin. The dogmas of the faith, the rules of ritual and worship, the civil and criminal law—all emanated from the same authority and were buttressed by the same ultimate sanctions. Those who were professionally expert in them followed different specializations in the same basic discipline of knowledge. That knowledge, in Arabic *Ilm,* was the preserve of the ulema—those who know. In Ottoman times their hierarchy was called *Ilmiye.*

The scholarship of the ulema was concerned with two main subjects, theology and law; their talents were exercised in two great professions, education and justice. The two were closely related, and indeed formed part of the same ladder of professional advancement. The holder of the highest offices were known as *Mollas,* an Arabic word meaning lord or master. It was applied to the chief religious dignitaries in the capital, and to the occupants of certain posts in other places, graded in rank and status.

In the strict theory of the Muslim jurists there is no legislative power in the state. God alone makes law, and promulgates it by revelation. The Holy Law of Islam, the *Shari'a,* thus rests on the Koran and on the traditions of the Prophet, as assembled and interpreted by the ancient doctors. The function of the sovereign is not to make or even to amend the law, which antedates and determines his own office, but to uphold and enforce it. The duty of the jurists similarly is not to revise or reform, still less to change the law, which is divine and eternal, but to expound and apply it.

The practical need to interpret and administer the law gave rather greater scope to the will of the sovereign and the skill of the lawyer than the strict letter of the law would suggest. The customary law of the peoples and provinces of the Empire often survived, to play no small part in the system of justice as actually administered; the will of the ruler, as expressed in decrees, dealt simply and efficiently with problems, notably financial and criminal matters, for which the treatises of the Holy Law provided no clear and immediate guidance. From time to time sets of rules were issued, known as *kanun,* and collected in *kanunnames,* some of them general, others dealing with particular areas or matters. These were not usually laws or enactments in the strict sense—rather tabulations, for administrative convenience, of existing law, and resting on *Shari'a,* custom, and decree. Many *kanuns* were promulgated during the reign of Süleyman the Magnificent, who is known in Ottoman annals as Süleyman Kanuni. The legal ulema were of two kinds—*kadis,* judges, and muftis, jurisconsults. The former, by far the more numerous in the Ottoman Empire, tried and adjudicated cases; the latter gave rulings, *fetva,* on points of law when consulted.

The first Ottoman ulema were scholars from the East, whom the sultans appointed as *kadis* in the various towns that they conquered. Murad I appointed a chief *kadi*, to whom he gave the title *kadi-asker*—*kadi* of the army. A second was appointed by Mehemmed II. From this beginning a great hierarchy of juridical-religious offices grew up, the like of which had never been known in Islamic history. At first it was headed by the two *kadi-askers;* then the chief mufti of Istanbul, who came to be known as the *Sheyh ül-Islam,* began to rise in power, and in the earty sixteenth century came to be acknowledged as the senior religious dignitary. His power and influence are expressed in the rules of court ceremonial; according to these he ranked immediately after the grand vizier, to whom alone he was required to pay courtesy calls. Later he seems to have ranked as the equal of the grand vizier, and even the sultan was required on occasion to pay him visits. His chief political function was to issue rulings—*fetva*—in accordance with the Islamic law, on questions of public policy. Thus he might be called upon to authorize a declaration of war, the deposition of the sultan, or to approve the issue of new rules and regulations. In the sixteenth century, when the Islamic influence was growing very rapidly, the chief muftis and their staffs played an important role in harmonizing the rules of the *Sharī'a* with the administrative practice of the Ottoman state.

He presided over a vast army of *kadis* and muftis with territorial jurisdictions like those of Christian justices and bishops. Also under his jurisdiction were the mosques, with their staffs of imams, muezzins, and preachers, and the schools, with their own hierarchy of schoolboys, students, tutors, teachers, professors, and principals. In these schools the bureaucratic as well as the religious classes received their education, and many of the high bureaucratic offices were normally held by members of the ulema class.

Many of the ulema were engaged in the teaching profession, at the summit of which were the senior professorships at the great medreses in Istanbul. Such were the great colleges founded by Mehemmed the Conqueror and Süleyman the Magnificent, as well as many lesser figures. Their syllabus consisted chiefly of religion and law, but also gave some—if dwindling—attention to the so-called rational sciences, such as natural history, astronomy, and mathematics. Medicine—of the medieval Islamic school—was also taught, and the profession of medicine was regarded as a branch of the *Ilmiye*. The professors of the medreses were graded in ranks, the highest of which were an acknowledged stage on the way to a judgeship or to one of the state offices, such as *nishanji* and defterdar, held by ulema. The *ḳadis*, though nominally judges, were also the keepers of many of the provincial records, and in the smaller provincial centers were in fact representatives of the executive power. The chief mufti had no temporal power; he could not initiate but only answer questions put to him. Nevertheless, as chief authorized exponent of the Holy Law, to which the sultan himself was subject, he enjoyed tremendous prestige; as head of an organized hierarchy he wielded great effective power.

This hierarchy enjoyed undisturbed control of law, justice, religion, and education. It also enjoyed financial independence. The ulema themselves were exempt from taxation, and, unlike their colleagues in the slave establishment, could transmit their possessions and even, in effect, their professional status from generation to generation, thus forming a real hereditary possessing class. Moreover, they were in effective control of the vast *wakf* revenues—lands or other revenue-producing properties consecrated as pious foundations for more or less religious purposes. These included of course many established for genuinely pious purposes; they also included a growing number of so-called civil or family *wakfs,* the enjoyment of which passed from father to son for generations with a degree of security unknown to any other form of tenure. In course of time vast properties became *wakf,* and their revenues were controlled by administrators appointed by and drawn from the ulema class. As Lady Wortley Montagu acutely remarked, in a letter of 1717:

> This set of men are equally capable of preferments in the law or the church, those two sciences being cast into one, and a lawyer and a priest being the same word in the Turkish language. They are the only men really considerable in the Empire, all the profitable employments and church revenues are in their hands. The Grand Signior, tho' general heir to his people, never presumes to touch their lands or money, which go, in an uninterrupted succession, to their children. 'Tis true, they lose this privilege by accepting a place at court, or the title of Bassa; but there are few examples of such fools among them. You may easily judge of the power of these men, who have engrossed all the learning, and almost all the wealth of the Empire.

In the early period the heads of the Ottoman ulema were often immigrants from countries of older Islamic civilization —from Persia and the Arab lands—or else had gone there for their education. By the sixteenth century however they consisted largely of Ottoman Turks, and disposed of their own centers of higher learning in the capital and the provincial centers. Despite the tendency for religious offices to become hereditary, they never became a closed priestly caste. Men of the second generation in the slave establishment—the sons of military and palace officers—often found a career in religion; also freeborn Muslims of humble origin—clerks and artisans, sometimes even tribesmen—found their way through the schools into the ranks of the ulema. Education, though far from universal, was free and endowed, and the promising student without means could rise through the ladder of the ulema class to the highest office.

The ulema were jurists and theologians, and their religion was legal, dogmatic, and severe. To the people, they appeared as judges and masters, powerful and often rich. Behind them were the majesty of the law and the might of the state, and a God who, even more than His representative the sultan, was immeasurably remote.

The ritual of the mosque is simple and austere. Orthodox Islam, like Christianity and Judaism, has rejected dancing from its worship and ritual. Going even further than its sister faiths, it has also rejected music and poetry, and confined its liturgy to a few simple, pious texts, taken chiefly from the Koran. The mosque has no altar and no sanctuary, for Islam has no sacraments or ordination. The Imam is neither priest nor pastor, but a leader in prayer. He may guide the believer in matters of religious law and ritual, but cannot interpose between him and God. Public prayer is a disciplined, corporate act of submission to the One, remote and transcendent God. It admits of no drama and no mystery, and has no place for liturgical music or poetry, still less for representational painting or sculpture, which Muslim piety rejects as blasphemy verging on idolatry. In their place Muslim artists used abstract designs, with elaborate decorative patterns based on sacred inscriptions in Arabic writing, mostly quotations from the Koran. In the hands of the great masters, calligraphy reached a summit of artistic achievement not easy of access for those brought up in another aesthetic and religious tradition.

The privileged aloofness of the orthodox ulema, the austerity of their worship, the cold legalism of their doctrines, failed to satisfy the spiritual and social needs of many Muslims, who turned elsewhere for sustenance and guidance. In earlier days, they had often followed the teachings of the Shi'a, regarded as heretical by the Sunni ulema, and many traces of Shi'ite belief still remained in popular religion. More important was the influence of the sufis, the mystics of Islam who since mediaeval times were organized in dervish brotherhoods, each dedicated to a different mystical way, called *tarikat*. These *tarikats* added much that was lacking in orthodox Islam. Dervish saints bridged the gap left by orthodoxy between man and God; dervish leaders served as pastors and guides; dervish meetings offered brotherhood and communion in the search for God and, on occasion, in the struggle for human needs. Their faith was warm, mystical, and intuitive; their worship was passionate and ecstatic, using music, song, and dance to bring the believer to mystical union with God. Unlike the ulema, the dervishes remained part of the people, wielding immense influence among them. In earlier days they were often leaders of movements of religious and social revolt—for charity and sanctity against legalism

and learning, for the people against the state and the hierarchy. At times they were able to penetrate even the palace
and the army themselves, and to challenge the ulema in the
very centers of power. They were present at the birth of the
Ottoman state, as religious mentors and preceptors of the
frontier warriors. They spread with the Turkish armies to the
newly conquered lands and cities, building up a far-flung
system of lodges and branches that came to include a large
part of the Turkish population. Their centers were the *tekke,*
a kind of cloister or convent where the *sheyh* of the order
resided, with a number of celibate followers. Married dervishes lived out and attended ceremonies at the *tekke,* as did
also the lay-brothers, called *muhibb,* lover (of God). Each
order had its own form of ecstatic worship, called *zikr,* and
its own discipline and rule. Some of their practices may well
retain traces of the dance cults of antiquity and the sham-
anistic rituals of the heathen Turks; some of their beliefs
reflect the impact of the Islamic heresies which the Turks
encountered on their way from Central Asia across Iran to
Anatolia, and which flourished in the relative freedom of the
Anatolian frontier. Yet another influence appears in the preservation, among converts to Islam, of some Christian beliefs,
and in the honor accorded, sometimes under disguised names,
to Christian saints, festivals, and holy places. The relative
importance of Turkish, local shi'ite, and Christian elements
in the faith and observances of the brotherhoods has been
variously assessed.

It is not surprising that the orthodox ulema regarded the
tarikats with suspicion, and not infrequently denounced
them. In particular they disliked their pantheistic doctrines,

which seemed to impugn the transcendental unity of God; their idolatrous worship of saints and holy places; their thaumaturgic practices and suspect methods of inducing ecstasy; their laxness in observing the divine law. Another ground for suspicion was the strong element of Shi'ism in the beliefs of almost all the brotherhoods—not enough, perhaps, to label them as Shi'a, but enough to arouse the fear and anger of Sunni orthodoxy. There were other fears, too, of the dangerous, pent-up energies which the dervish leaders controlled, and could, if they desired, release. Under both Seljuk and Ottoman rule, the dervishes led numerous rebellions, in the name of religious ideals, and at times offered a deadly threat to the established order. The first great dervish rising was that of Baba Ishak, in the thirteenth century. Another, led by the famous Sheyh Bedr ed-Din, almost destroyed the Ottoman Empire before being crushed in 1416. In 1519, Selim I, following his victories against Persia and Egypt, had to suppress a rebel called Jelali, with messianic pretensions, in the neighborhood of Tokat; in 1527, Süleyman the Magnificent, soon after his triumph over the Hungarians at Mohács, had to send the grand vizier with an army to Anatolia, to crush a rebellion in Karaman led by a dervish known as Kalender oglu, and claiming descent from Hajji Bektash. Yet another series of risings followed in the late sixteenth and early seventeenth centuries, one of them, in 1608, led by another Kalender oglu, called Mehmed Aga.

Kalender oglu means son of a Kalender, a familiar figure in the writings of the early European travellers to the Ottoman Empire, as well as in the stories of the *Thousand and One Nights*. The Kalenders were wandering mendicant dervishes, who deliberately flouted Muslim opinion by shaving their beards, hair, and eyebrows and by throwing off the restraints of the Holy Law and most others. The term *Baba* —father—was applied to dervish leaders generally, and particularly to those who, from the eleventh century onwards, inspired the Turkish frontiersmen and tribesmen who conquered and colonized Anatolia.

It was from these circles that the first great Turkish brotherhood, that of the Bektashi dervishes, emerged. Their patron and eponymous founder was Hajji Bektash, an immigrant from Khurasan who was probably a disciple of Baba Ishak, leader of the Anatolian rebellion of 1240. The order drew its inspiration from various sources, Central Asian and local, and, after a long development in the course of which it absorbed considerable Christian elements, seems to have reached its classical form at the beginning of the sixteenth century. Their Grand Master, or *Chelebi,* resided at the mother convent by the tomb of Hajji Bektash, between Kayseri and Kirshehir; their branches spread over Anatolia and Rumelia. They soon established themselves in the capital where, at the time of their dissolution in 1826, they were reported as having fourteen convents. According to an old legend, Hajji Baktash was the founder of the corps of Janissaries, to whom he gave their name and distinctive headdress. Though certainly untrue in this form, the story probably reflects an early link between the corps and the Anatolian dervishes. In the fifteenth and sixteenth centuries the Bektashis acquired a dominant influence over the religious life of the Janissaries, serving as preceptors and chaplains to their cadets and soldiers and giving them the character of a religious-military fraternity.

In spite of their connection with the Janissaries, the Bektashis retained something of their popular and radical character, and frequently aroused the suspicion of the state and the ulema. A story told by the historian Esad Efendi at the time of their dissolution is very revealing, if not of the attitudes of the Bektashis themselves, then of the charges brought against them by their opponents. In 1690, he says, during the war with Austria,

> an accursed Bektashi went among the Muslim troops when they were encamped for the night and went from soldier to soldier saying: "Hey, you fools, why do you squander your lives for nothing? Fie on you! All the talk you hear about the virtues of holy war and martyrdom in battle is so much nonsense. While the Ottoman Emperor enjoys himself in his palace, and the Frankish king disports himself in his country, I can't think why you should give your lives fighting on these mountain-tops!"

In spite of such accusations, of frequent charges of heresy, impiety and, what was worse, of sedition, the Bektashis continued to flourish, their connection with the corps of Janissaries assuring them of a position of power and influence at the very center of the Ottoman state.

It was perhaps in order to counteract this influence that the Ottoman authorities gave some encouragement to another, rival *tarikat,* which also came to play a major role in the life of the Ottoman Empire. This was the great brotherhood of the Mevlevis, known to the West as the Dancing Dervishes. Their name comes from the famous mystic and poet Jelal ed-Din Rumi, known as *Mevlana,* "our lord," who lived in the Seljuk capital of Konya, in the thirteenth century.

Their Western name derives from part of the discipline of the *zikr,* when they whirled round and round on the right foot, to the music of reed flutes and other instruments, until they achieved ecstasy. The Grand Master of the order, the *Chelebi,* resided at Konya, in the central convent by the tomb of their eponymous founder. The Mevlevis were the nearest to ortho- doxy among the *tarikats.* Their following was urban and mid- dle or upper class, and included many famous Turkish poets and musicians; their doctrines were sophisticated, and could be so presented as to minimize their divergence from ortho- doxy. By the end of the sixteenth century they had won the favor of the sultans, and in 1648 their Grand Master officiated, for the first time, at the ceremony of the girding on of the sword of Osman, which marked the accession of a new sultan. Later Grand Masters sometimes exercised the same privilege.

The Bektashis and Mevlevis were both of Anatolian Turk- ish origin, and in the main restricted to territories subject to Ottoman rule or influence. Other orders were introduced from elsewhere in the Islamic world. Such for example were the Kadiris, founded in Iraq in the twelfth century, and prob- ably the oldest surviving dervish brotherhood. This compara- tively orthodox order seems to have been introduced into Turkey at the time of the Ottoman conquest of Iraq in the sixteenth century, and was soon strongly established in Istan- bul. Another and earlier importation from Iraq was the *tari- kat* of the Rifais, known in the West as the Howling Der- vishes. Their followers stabbed, gashed, and burned them- selves without suffering injury, and practiced a *zikr* based on rhythmic shouts and cries.

The Nakshbendi order was of Central Asian origin; it is

said to have been introduced in Turkey in the late fifteenth century by the poet Ilahi, who visited the tomb of the founder in Bukhara, was initiated into the order, and brought a Bukharan *sheyh* back with him to Istanbul, where he set up the first Nakshbendi lodge in Turkey. Several Turkish authors of the time were among the disciples of the Nakshbendi order, notably the poet and mystic Lamii of Bursa (d.1531), author of innumerable works in verse and prose. At a later date the Nakshbendi order was reintroduced from India in a more militant form, and acquired a considerable lay following. Its beliefs were closer to Sunni orthodoxy than those of most of the other orders, and its followers were strict in their observance of the prayers, fasts, and other observances prescribed by the Holy Law. Evliya Chelebi, writing after the middle of the seventeenth century, recognizes the importance of the Nakshbendis, and remarks that "the great *Sheyhs* may be classed in two principal orders; that of the Halveti and that of the Nakshbendi."

The Halveti order, which Evliya Chelebi also mentions, was for a while of special importance. Its name comes from the Arabic word *Khalwa,* meaning solitude, and refers to the rule of the order which required members to go once a year into solitary retreat for up to forty days in a cell, fasting and praying from dawn to dusk. The order was founded in the first half of the fifteenth century by a mystical Sheyh of Shemakha, in the eastern Caucasus. It soon won a following among the Turcoman tribes of Azerbayjan and eastern Turkey, and was carried westward by a group of active and devoted missionaries. Very soon after the capture of Istanbul, the Halvetis were strongly established there, under a leader who enjoyed great influence and authority among the people. The militant attitude, extensive following, political ambitions and dubious orthodoxy of the Halvetis made them an object of recurring suspicion to both the Sultan and the ulema. Mehemmed the Conqueror soon "advised" the Halveti leader to leave the city, but the order was already well entrenched, and able to play a considerable if rather obscure political role under several of his successors.

During the early seventeenth century a series of significant clashes occurred between the Halvetis and their orthodox opponents. The two opposing leaders were the Halveti *Sheyh* Sivasi Efendi (d.1639) and the orthodox preacher and teacher Mehmed Efendi, usually known as Kadizade, "the *Kadi's* son" (d.1635–6). The rivalry between the two was well described by their contemporary, the famous Kâtib Chelebi:

> These two sheyhs were diametrically opposed to one another; because of their differing temperaments, warfare arose between them. In most . . . controversies . . . Kadizade took one side and Sivasi took the other, both going to extremes, and the followers of both used to quarrel and dispute, one against the other. For many years this situation continued, with disputation raging between the two parties, and out of the futile quarrelling a mighty hatred and hostility arose between them. The majority of sheyhs took one side or the other, though the intelligent ones kept out of it, saying, "This is a profitless quarrel, born of fanaticism. We are all members of the community of Muhammad, brothers in faith. We have no warrant from Sivasi, no diploma from Kadizade, They are simply a couple of reverend sheyhs who have won fame by opposing one another; their fame has even reached the ear of the Sultan. Thus

have they secured their own advantage and basked in the sunshine of the world. Why should we be so foolish as to fight their battles for them? We shall get no joy of it."

But some foolish people persistently attached themselves to one side or the other, hoping to become famous like them. When the cut and thrust of verbal contention from their several pulpits was near to bringing them into real warfare with sword and spear, it became necessary for the Sultan to discipline some of them and administer a box on the ears in the shape of banishment from the city. It is among the duties of the Sultan of the Muslims to subdue and discipline ranting fanatics of this sort, whoever they may be, for in the past manifold corruption has come about from such militant bigotry.

These conflicts were based on something more than personal rivalries and jealousies, however, and continued long after the deaths of both protagonists. A little later in the century a notable battle was fought over coffee and tobacco, which the dervishes defended and which the orthodox condemned, together with music and dancing, as impious and licentious. The struggle between mystics and dogmatists was a principal theme in the religious life of the Ottoman Empire, and has not entirely ceased even at the present day.

What Christianity was to Europe, Islam was to the Ottoman Empire; what Latin and Greek were to European culture, the Arabic and Persian classics of Islam were to the culture of the Ottoman Turks. Ottoman literature is essentially an Islamic literature, written for the most part in the Turkish language, but in the Arabic script, with an immense borrowing of Arabic and Persian words, notions, and themes. In theology and law, Arabic influences predominated. Many Ottoman ulema were men of Arab origin, and some even who were not used the Arabic language in preference to Turkish as their medium of expression. In poetry and polite letters it was Iran rather than Arabia that provided the models of Ottoman style and elegance; the Persian classics were read, studied, translated and imitated in Turkey, and a knowledge of them was considered an essential part of the equipment of a scholar or man of letters.

This does not mean that Ottoman literature was purely derivative and imitative. The great Turkish writers succeeded in adapting and recreating the Perso-Arabic tradition as something new, significant, and vital. A few brief excerpts may serve as illustrations of two areas, poetry and history, in which Turkish writers most excelled.

The poet Mesihi was born in Albania, and went to Istanbul in his youth as a theological student. He won some reputation as a calligrapher and poet, but was unable to recover from the setback to his career following the death of his patron. He withdrew from the city to a small fief in Bosnia, where he died in 1512. Ottoman opinion regarded him as the greatest lyric poet before Baki. The best known of his poems in the West is his ode to the spring; a translation, into elegant eighteenth-century verse, was published by Sir William Jones in 1774.

> Hear how the nightingales, on every spray,
> Hail in wild notes the sweet return of May!
> The gale, that o'er yon waving almond blows,
> The verdant bank with silver blossoms strows:
> The smiling season decks each flowery glade
> Be gay: too soon the flowers of Spring will fade.

What gales of fragrance scent the vernal air!
Hills, dales, and woods, their loveliest mantles wear.
Who knows, what cares await that fatal day,
When ruder gusts shall banish gentle May?
Ev'n death, perhaps, our valleys will invade.
Be gay: too soon the flowers of Spring will fade.

The tulip now its varied hue displays,
And sheds, like Ahmed's eye, celestial rays.
Ah, nation ever faithful, ever true,
The joys of youth, while May invites, pursue!
Will not these notes your timorous minds persuade?
Be gay: too soon the flowers of Spring will fade.

The sparkling dewdrops o'er the lilies play,
Like orient pearls, or like the beams of day.
If love and mirth your wanton thoughts engage,
Attend, ye nymphs! (a poet's words are sage).
While thus you sit beneath the trembling shade,
Be gay: too soon the flowers of Spring will fade.

The fresh blown rose like Zeineb's cheek appears,
When pearls, like dewdrops, glitter in her ears.
The charms of youth at once are seen and past;
And nature says, "They are too sweet to last."
So blooms the rose; and so the blushing maid!
Be gay: too soon the flowers of Spring will fade.

See yon anemonies their leaves unfold,
With rubies flaming, and with living gold!
While crystal showers from weeping clouds descend,
Enjoy the presence of thy tuneful friend.
Now, while the wines are brought, the sofa's lay'd,
Be gay: too soon the flowers of Spring will fade.

The plants no more are dried, the meadows dead,
No more the rose-bud hangs her pensive head:
The shrubs revive in valleys, meads, and bowers,
And every stalk is diadem'd with flowers;
In silken robes each hillock stands array'd.
Be gay: too soon the flowers of Spring will fade.

Clear drops each morn impearl the rose's bloom,
And from its leaf the Zephyr drinks perfume;
The dewy buds expand their lucid store:
Be this our wealth: ye damsels, ask no more.
Though wise men envy and though fools upbraid,
Be gay: too soon the flowers of Spring will fade.

The dewdrops, sprinkled by the musky gale,
Are chang'd to essence ere they reach the dale.
The mild blue sky a rich pavilion spreads,
Without our labour, o'er our favour'd heads.
Let others toil in war, in arts, or trade.
Be gay: too soon the flowers of Spring will fade.

Late gloomy winter chill'd the sullen air,
Till Soliman arose, and all was fair.
Soft in his reign the notes of love resound,
And pleasure's rosy cup goes freely round.
Here on the bank, which mantling vines o'ershade,
Be gay: too soon the flowers of Spring will fade.

May this rude lay from age to age remain,
A true memorial of this lovely train.
Come, charming maid, and hear thy poet sing,
Thyself the rose, and He the bird of spring:
Love bids him sing, and Love will be obey'd.
Be gay: too soon the flowers of Spring will fade.

By common consent the greatest Turkish poet of his time
was Baki (1526–1600). Born in Istanbul, the son of a muezzin, he was at first apprenticed to a saddler, but began to study
at a medrese, where his talents won him the attention and
encouragement of some of the greatest scholars and writers of
his day and an entry to the ranks of the ulema. In 1555 he
presented an ode to Sultan Süleyman the Magnificent, who
had just returned from his Persian campaign. The ensuing
success won him the favor and friendship of the Sultan, who
even sent him his own verses for correction, and opened the
way to a brilliant religious and literary career. The death of
Süleyman was a grievous blow to him, and he mourned his
friend and benefactor in a famous elegy, which is regarded
as his finest work. The poet begins with a traditional theme,
reminding the reader or listener of the impermanence of
worldly pomp, and urging him, if he has forgotten this, to
see what has befallen the great Süleyman:

> Oh you, whose foot is caught in the snare of fame and glory,
> How long will you covet the things of this restless world?
>
> Think of that day when, at the end of the spring of life,
> The tulip-coloured face will turn into an autumn leaf.
>
> For you, as for the dregs in the cup, earth must be the last
>   dwelling;
> The stone from the hand of time must strike the cup of life.
>
> He is a man indeed whose heart is clear as a mirror.
> If you are a man, why should the tiger's spite be in your breast?
>
> Till when will the sleep of neglect lie on the eye of experience?
> Are you not content with what has befallen the emperor,
>   the lion of war?

That master-rider of the realm of bliss
For whose careering steed the field of the world was narrow.

The infidels of Hungary bowed their heads to the
    temper of his blade,
The Frank admired the grain of his sword.

He laid his face to the ground, graciously, like a fresh rose petal,
The treasurer of time put him in the coffer, like a jewel.

. . .

The day is born. Will not the lord of the world
    awake from sleep?
Does he not show himself from his pavilion,
    that is like the heavens?

Our eyes are on the roads, no word has come
From the place where lies the dust beneath the threshold
    of his majesty.

The colour of his cheek has gone, he lies dry-lipped
Like a fallen rose apart from the rose water.

Sometimes the Emperor of the skies hides behind the
    curtain of cloud,
When he remembers your grace he sweats with shame
    from the cloud.

This is my prayer: all those who do not weep for you,
Young and old, may their tears be buried in the ground.

May the sun burn and blaze with the fire of your parting;
In grief for you, let him dress in black weeds of cloud.

Weeping tears of blood as it recalls your skill,
May your sword plunge into the ground from its scabbard.

May the pen tear its collar in grief for you,
The standard rend its shirt in affliction.

Two examples must suffice from the vast and rich literature of Ottoman historiography. The first is a victory letter—a well-known genre in Ottoman literature. The victory letter was an elaborate literary composition; its purpose was to describe and still more to celebrate a victory won by land or sea by the sultan's armed forces, and thus to encourage his friends and overawe his enemies. Copies of it were sent to friendly and some other sovereigns, and often it was transcribed into the chronicles of the Empire.

A good example of this genre, halfway between political propaganda and heroic saga, is the victory bulletin of Kanisza, written to commemorate the capture of that fortress from the Hapsburgs by the Ottomans in 1600. Its author was probably the great historian Hasanbeyzade, then serving as *Reis Efendi;* the text is found in a letter from Istanbul to Queen Elizabeth of England, and preserved in the Public Record Office in London:

> Be it known that in this auspicious year we set forth with our mighty and illustrious soldiers from Belgrade, the House of the Holy War. While we were on the way to Buda, the brigands of the enemy fortresses called Babocza and Kanizsa burnt the bridges on the road to Buda and oppressed the people and the nobles with the fire of tyranny. Since it was agreed to be a necessary and important matter and an obligatory and ordained deed to eliminate them, the bridle of movement was guided to that quarter and the reins of activity were directed towards conquering and seizing the said fortresses. First we reached the fortress of Babocza. We set up our magnificent encampment all around it. The licentious ones confined within could not resist the necessarily victorious attack of our van.

As they surrendered the fortress within two days, we left that place and invested the fortress of Kanizsa, which is the key to the lands of the base infidels, the strong wall and iron gate of the realms of the ill-fated Hungarians. But since there was a strongly fortified water-tower attached to this fortress, and around it a rampart with turrets reaching the crown of the sun and with towers the tops of which joined the chambered firmament, it could not be stormed, neither could it be undermined. Having set up thunderous cannon in various places, so that the tumult of battle reached the ethereal spheres, and having covered the marsh with beams and erected wood-piles like mountains about its four sides, we launched the assault on the 28th day of the month of Rebi ül-Evvel. Meanwhile the king of Vienna—with . . . his renowned commanders celebrated for counsel and courage, and with more than 100,000 foot and horse of the vain infidels, with stores and weapons without reckoning, in fine with vehicles and tents and pavilions without end—approached our imperial and victorious army. Commencing the battle, the victorious soldiers of Islam knew those days as days of festival; without fear or foreboding they were agile and swift; and went to meet the enemy. The fires of battle were kindled on both sides, and mighty war and slaughter took place. On that day there was great glory. . . .

Our victorious soldiers, for three whole days, on one side bombarded the fortress, on the other waged war and battle against the infidel camp. But the accursed evildoers dug deep trenches around their camps, and set up cannon about them. On the fourth day the ranks and columns met again, right, left, centre and flanks were swiftly ordered. Several thousand foot and horse were driven back from various places to their camp, and numberless firearms were set up against it. Cannon-balls and musket shot were showered on their heads like rain and hail. Our victory-distinguished soldiers attacked them on every side like a deluge of destruction. On the morning of the seventh day, with the help of God the conquering King, the gates of victory were opened. The foe, foredoomed to defeat, was unable to hold firm. Falling and rising, they were driven back to the place whence they had come. The Gazis, ordained to conquer, followed their rear. Several thousand foot and horse became food for the sword and several thousand became captives and prisoners. All their cannon, munitions, powder, magazines and grain were taken. . . . The licentious ones still surrounded in the fortress, as an animal about to be slaughtered struggles, put forward the foot of obstinacy and persisted in stubbornness and arrogance. As a drowning man attempts everything, they exerted every effort and began to discharge whatever stones and beams and muskets and cannon they could find. Again without delay we shot at them cannons and muskets and arrows and other weapons of war, by night and day we advanced step by step. They realised that the assault was being prepared and understood that unless the strong fortress was surrendered they could not escape the irresistible talons. Therefore perforce they surrendered on the 13th day of the month of Rebi ül-Akhir. They knocked on the door of mercy and begged for pardon and generosity. They handed over the keys of the fortress . . . and quarter was given to their lives and property and to their children and wives. They were sent home. . . . Praise be to Almighty God, in this blessed year . . . such glorious deeds have come to pass. May all our foes be conquered and broken in this wise.

The second extract deals not with war but with diplomacy, and shows the Ottoman historian in a very different mood. This passage, dealing with the reception in Istanbul in 1653

of an ambassador from the Mogul Emperor of India and the
appointment of a return embassy, was written by a contemporary historian and preserved by the imperial historiographer
Naima. It well illustrates the sophisticated and urbane Istanbul society of the time:

> On 23rd Rejeb he came to the divan and presented his gifts.
> They included three valuable presents, of an estimated com-
> bined value of 300,000 piastres—a turban-crest with a diamond
> bigger than the Sultan's, a sword, and a dagger. Since the am-
> bassador was one of the ulema, the vizier, the Mufti, the Kadi-
> askers and other high dignitaries all gave receptions in his
> honour, at which learned and worthy men, masters of the arts
> of conversation, were present, and entertained the ambassador
> with scholarly discussion and witty repartee. These receptions
> were held in world-adorning palaces and in heart-delighting
> waterside pavilions, so as to show him the strange and won-
> drous sights of Istanbul. Indeed, it has never been heard that
> an ambassador has been received with so much attention and
> deference. After the ambassador had been treated with full
> honours, a letter of reply was written to the Emperor of India.
> An emerald-hilted dagger, twenty beautiful slave-girls and a
> finely caparisoned horse, whose trappings were estimated to
> be worth 90 purses, were given as gifts to the Emperor, while
> the ambassador was given 6000 pieces of gold, a fur robe, and
> a caparisoned horse. A meeting was held to choose an ambassa-
> dor to accompany him back to India. According to ancient cus-
> tom it would have been proper to send a man of experience
> from among the ulema or scribes, or else a man of eloquence
> from among the scholars and literati. In fact however, these
> necessary qualifications were disregarded. Zulfikar Aga, the
> brother of Salih Pasha, asked for this embassy, saying: "I need

no expenses. I will pay for it out of my own pocket." Deeming this arrangement both advantageous and suitable—on the principle that a cheap hire makes a suitable companion—they appointed this ignorant Bosniak as ambassador.

His Majesty the Sultan, having heard of the excellence of the Indian ambassador and of his brilliant conversation . . . said: "Let a learned and able man be appointed as ambassador, for ambassadors are the honour of kings." The vizier and the mufti held counsel on whom to appoint. Certain learned men were put forward, whereupon someone said: "If you appoint a man of culture and discernment, then besides his travel expenses he will require a personal allowance, and will pester and burden us with claims and demands for attention."

With this in mind, they decided on Zulfikar Aga, and said to him: "Call on the ambassador . . . give him a fine reception, be friendly and sociable, but in company keep silent. Don't feel that you have to talk, and then commit some gross error." This is how they instructed him. This ass then set out with indescribable pomp to call on the ambassador, inform him of his own appointment, and invite him to a reception. The late Manoglu says that of the literary set he invited no one, of the poets only Jevri Chelebi, and of the wits of Kadizade's following, Ebu Ahmed-oglu. These two men were friends of his, confidants and intimates; they were to entertain the ambassador, and also to use their skill to cover up his own blunders, if he made any.

Zulifikar Aga gave a fine reception, where, among other dishes, he had ordered two or three dishes made from cabbage, which he regarded as the greatest of delicacies. The ambassador came and sat down, and in due course, after many social solecisims, dinner was served. When the cabbage was brought,

Zulfikar turned to the ambassador and asked: "Are there any cabbages in India?" The ambassador replied that "Cold plants of no special quality are very rarely cultivated in temperate climates."

Zulfikar, not understanding what the ambassador had said, went on:

"Sir, this is a useful thing. It strengthens a man's spirits."

The ambassador smiled, and remarked: "There is no doubt that it is a cause of wind, but apart from this verbal affinity I do not know of any connection with spirits." Zulfikar understood neither the sense of the ambassador's words nor the reason for his smile. Stupidly imitating him, he also uttered a guffaw and said:

"Sir, your joke is very good, but it is a fact that the Albanians are clever because they eat pluck (*chiger*) while the Bosniaks are strong and brave because they eat cabbage."

The ambassador, somewhat put out, retorted: "According to the principle you have laid down, the Albanians ought to be plucky (*chigerdar*) and the Bosniaks windy."

Jevri and Ebu Ahmed, who understood the point of his remarks, were bursting with involuntary laughter, but were ashamed to do so over the food. Forcing back their laughter, they could not even eat.

The tables were cleared, and the reception came to an end. When the ambassador was about to go, Zulfikar said to him: "Please God, we shall enjoy our journey in the company of your excellency." To which the ambassador replied: "Yes, on the way we shall observe some very strange things, and be diverted by them; may Almighty God in any case keep us safe and sound." He then arose, remarking: "Praise be to God, who created an ox in the form of a man! It is a fine companion whose company we shall enjoy."—and went to his place.

The party having dispersed, Zulfikar detained Jevri and Ebu Ahmed-oglu, and said to them:

"Didn't I talk properly to that pander? They brag about their cinnamon and cloves, but if we didn't buy their goods who would? Let us also take pride in the products of our country. He talked to me in fancy language, but I talked back well enough in plain Turkish."

Since, as he was a wealthy man and an ambassador designate, it was not proper to put him to shame, and since equally he lacked the capacity to be taught or made to understand, they found no way but to remain silent. . . .

Ebu Ahmed-oglu gave an account of the affair to Manoglu, who was a friend of his. "Looking at it impartially," he asked "at a time when ulema and scribes and men of letters are available, is it proper to send such common fellows on embassies, just because of their money? Are such scandals compatible with the preservation of the honour and reputation of the Empire?"

Epilogue

In 1630, Kochu Bey, a palace official of Balkan extraction, presented a memorandum to Sultan Murad IV in which he examines, for his master's guidance, the weaknesses in Ottoman State and Society that had led to a decline in Ottoman power since the days of Süleyman the Magnificent, and makes suggestions on how to put them right:

> It is a long time since the high-chambered household of the lofty Sultanate (may it remain under the protection of eternal grace) was served by solicitous, well-intentioned, worthy ulema and by obedient, self-effacing, willing slaves. Today the state of affairs having changed, and evil, tumult, sedition and dissension having passed all bounds, I have sought occasion to observe the causes and reasons of those changes, and to bring them to the Imperial and August ear. . . . First, let it be known to his Imperial Majesty that the origin of the good order of kingship and community and the cause of the stability of the foundations of the faith and the dynasty are a firm grasp of

the strong cord of the Muhammadan law. For the rest, let the Imperial attention and favour be given to the men of religion, who with care and knowledge attend to the affairs of the subjects entrusted to the Emperor by God, and to the soldiers who give up their lives in the Holy War. Let him show favour to the worthy men of every class, and contempt for the unworthy.

Kochu Bey depicts the glorious apogee of Ottoman greatness under Süleyman the Magnificent in glowing words—but is careful to point out that it was in his reign that the first signs of weakness appeared, which led to so rapid a deterioration under his successors. He attributes this decline to a series of interrelated causes. The first was the withdrawal of the Sultan from the effective control of public affairs, thus breaking off the indispensable intimacy between the source of power and those entrusted with its exercise. The second was the degradation of the office of grand vizier, who instead of rising, as formerly, through the ladder of administrative experience and personal merit, was now appointed—and manipulated—by palace favor. Without competence or dignity, he was liable at any moment to summary dismissal or even execution, and thus brought his own great office into disrepute. With an absent Sultan and a courtier grand vizier, the way was open to the domination of the harem—to government by women, eunuchs, parasites, speculators and hangers-on of all kinds. Even the Imperial Household and the corps of Janissaries were contaminated:

> Into the Imperial Harem, contrary to the law, have come
> . . . men with no religion and no faith, tricksters and topers
> and city riff-raff of no known nation or religion, Turcomans,
> gypsies, Tats, Kurds, foreigners, Lazes, nomads, muleteers and

camel-drivers, porters, syrup-vendors, footpads and cutpurses and all kinds of others, so that order and discipline have been ruined, laws and standards have ceased to exist. . . .

The regime of irresponsible favorites had in turn opened the way to corruption, the blight which, if unchecked, would destroy every branch of the Ottoman social and political order. Appointments and promotions were obtained by favor or purchase; the tenure of office was brief and insecure, the holders incompetent and unworthy.

Writing little more than half a century after the death of Süleyman, Kochu Bey could still think of the preceding period as an evil interlude, and could hope that swift and resolute action would stop the decay and restore the greatness of the Empire:

And then the enemies of the faith, seeing the good order and stability, will say, in helpless fear and envy: "The House of Osman lay for sixty years in neglectful sleep, but now they are wide awake, and have begun to make good the short-comings of past days."

But despite some intervals of revival, the decline continued, and gradually a more pessimistic note begins to be heard in the writings of later memorialists. "As I knew that my recommendations would be difficult to apply," wrote Kâtib Chelebi, speaking of his own memorandum on reform of 1653, "I took no further trouble about it. But a Sultan of some future time will become aware of it, and put those measures into operation, which will bring him the best results."

Ottoman statesmen and writers of the seventeenth and eighteenth centuries were still looking backward to a golden age in the past, and saw the only hope of saving the Empire in a restoration of the faith and law of Islam and a return to the pure and ancient traditions of the house of Osman. In 1792, when Sultan Selim III asked a score of eminent Ottomans for their advice on how to save the Empire, there were many who still gave the same answer. There were some, however, who had found a new way—the way of reform and renewal by which, in time, the Turkish people were to pass through the final collapse of the Ottoman Empire to the birth of the Turkish Republic.

Bibliography

Works on Ottoman History and Institutions

Babinger, Franz. *Mehmed der Eroberer und seine Zeit: Weltenstürmer einer Zeitenwende.* Munich, 1953. French and Italian translations.

Gibb, H. A. R., and Harold Bowen. *Islamic Society and the West.* Vol. I, *Islamic Society in the Eighteenth Century.* 2 parts. London, 1950–57.

Hammer-Purgstall, Joseph, *freiherr* von. *Geschichte des osmanischen Reiches.* 10 vols. Pest, 1827–35. 2nd ed., 4 vols., 1834–36; French translation, *Histoire de l'Empire ottoman,* 18 vols., Paris, 1835–43.

Iorga, Nicolae. *Geschichte des osmanischen Reiches.* 5 vols. Gotha, 1908–13.

Köprülü, Mehmet Fuat. *Les origines de l'empire ottoman.* Paris, 1935.

Lane-Poole, Stanley. *Turkey.* London, 1888.

Lewis, Bernard. *The Emergence of Modern Turkey.* London, 1961.

Lybyer, A. H. *The Government of the Ottoman Empire in the time of the Suleiman the Magnificent.* Cambridge, Mass., 1913.

Miller, Barnette. *The Palace School of Muhammad the Conqueror.* Cambridge, Mass., 1941.

Pears, Edwin. *The Destruction of the Greek Empire.* London, 1903.

Vaughan, Dorothy. *Europe and the Turk: A Pattern of Alliances, 1350–1700.* Liverpool, 1954.

Wittek, Paul. *The Rise of the Ottoman Empire.* London, 1938.

Zinkeisen, J. W. *Geschichte des osmanischen Reiches in Europa.* 8 vols. Hamburg, 1840–63.

WORKS ON OTTOMAN LITERATURE, SCIENCE, AND ART

[Adivar], Abdülhak Adnan. *La Science chez les turcs ottomans.* Paris, 1939.

Arseven, C. E. *L'Art turc.* Istanbul, 1939.

Bombaci, Alessio. *Storia della letteratura turca dall'antico impero di Mongolia all'odierna Turchia.* Milan, 1956.

Gibb, E. J. W. *A History of Ottoman Poetry.* 6 vols. London, 1900–1909.

UNESCO. *Turkey: Ancient Minatures.* New York, 1961.

Ünsal, Behcet. *Turkish Islamic Architecture.* London, 1959.

WORKS ON ISTANBUL

Gabriel, Albert. "Les Mosquées de Constantinople," in *Syria* (1926), 353–419.

Gurlitt, Cornelius. *Die Baukunst Konstantinopels.* 2 vols. Berlin, 1872.

Liddell, Robert. *Byzantium and Istanbul.* London, 1956.

Mamboury, Ernest. *Istanbul touristique.* Istanbul, 1951.

Mayer, Robert. *Byzantion Konstantinupolis Istanbul.* Vienna, 1943.

TRANSLATIONS OF OTTOMAN WORKS

Ashikpashazade. *Vom Hirtenzelt zur hohen Pforte.* Trans. by R. F. Kreutel. Graz, 1959.

Evliya Chelebi. *Narrative of Travels in Europe, Asia, and Africa.* Trans by J. von Hammer. London, 1834.

————. *Im Reiche des goldenen Apfels.* Trans. by R. F. Kreutel. Graz, 1957.

Kâtib Chelebi. *The Balance of Truth.* Trans. by G. L. Lewis. London, 1957.

Mesihi, in *The Works of Sir William Jones,* X, 271–76. London, 1807.

Naima. *Annals of the Turkish Empire.* Trans. by Charles Fraser. London, 1832.

Sad ed-Din. *The Capture of Constantinople.* Trans. by E. J. W. Gibb. London, 1879.

WESTERN TRAVELERS CITED IN THE TEXT

Busbecq, Ogier Ghiselin de. *The Turkish Letters* .... Trans. by C. T. Forster and F. H. B. Daniell. 2 vols. London, 1881. The citation is from an earlier English version published in London in 1694.

Dallam, Thomas. *Diary,* in *Early Voyages and Travels in the Levant.* Ed. by J. Theodore Bent. London, 1893.

Hakluyt, Richard. *The Principal Navigations, Voyages, Traffiques and Discoveries of the English Nation* .... London, 1589. Vols. 5 and 8 reprinted in Glasgow, 1904.

Langusto, Giacomo, cited in Thomas, "Die Eroberung Constantinopels im Jahre 1453 aus einer venetianischen Chronik," *S. B. der Kgl. bayerischen Akad. der Wiss.* Munich, 1868.

Montagu, Lady Mary Wortley. *Letters.* London, 1763.

Most Rare and Straunge Discourses, of Amurathe the Turkish Emperor that nowe is. London, n.d.

Rycaut, Sir Paul. *The History of the present State of the Ottoman Empire.* London, 1668.

Sanderson, John. *Travels . . . in the Levant.* Ed. by Sir William Foster. London, 1931.

Withers, Robert. *A Description of the Grand Signior's Serraglio* (after Ottaviano Bon), in *Purchas His Pilgrimage: Or, Relations of the World and Religions Observed in all Ages and Places discovered, from the creation unto this present.* 4 parts. London, 1625. Reprinted in Glasgow, 1905, IX, 322ff. A slightly different version was published by John Greaves, *Miscellaneous tracts . . .*, London, 1650, and there have been later reprints.

BIBLIOGRAPHIES

American Historical Association. *Guide to Historical Literature,* 366ff. New York, 1961.

Birge, J. K. *A Guide to Turkish Area Study.* Washington, 1949.

Pearson, J. D. *Index Islamicus 1906–1955.* Cambridge, 1958.

———. *Index Islamicus Supplement 1956–1960.* Cambridge, 1962.

Sauvaget, Jean. *Introduction à l'histoire de l'orient musulman,* 195–220. Rev. by Claude Cahen. Paris, 1961.

Weber, Shirley. *Voyages and Travels in Greece, the Near East and Adjacent Regions.* 2 vols. Princeton, N. J., 1952–53.

Index

Index

THE CENTERS OF CIVILIZATION SERIES, of which this volume is the ninth, is intended to include accounts of the great cities of the world during particular periods of their flowering, from ancient times to the present. The following list is complete as of the date of printing of this volume:

16. Gaston Wiet. *Cairo: City of Art and Commerce.* Translated by Seymour Feiler.
17. Douglas Young. *Edinburgh in the Age of Sir Walter Scott.*
18. Richard Nelson Frye. *Bukhara: The Medieval Achievement.*
19. Walter Muir Whitehill. *Boston in the Age of John Fitzgerald Kennedy.*
20. Arthur J. May. *Vienna in the Age of Franz Josef.*
21. John J. Murray. *Amsterdam in the Age of Rembrandt.*
22. Wendell Cole. *Kyoto in the Momoyama Period.*
23. Aldon D. Bell. *London in the Age of Charles Dickens.*
24. John Griffiths Pedley. *Sardis in the Age of Croesus.*
25. W. W. Robinson. *Los Angeles: A Profile.*
26. George C. Rogers, Jr. *Charleston in the Age of the Pinckneys.*
27. John J. Murray. *Antwerp in the Age of Plantin and Breughel.*
28. Gaston Wiet. *Baghdad: Metropolis of the Abbasid Caliphate.* Translated by Seymour Feiler.
29. William R. Tyler. *Dijon and the Valois Dukes of Burgundy.*
30. Barisa Krekic. *Dubrovnik in the Fourteenth and Fifteenth Centuries: A City Between East and West.*
31. Alec R. Myers. *London in the Age of Chaucer.*
32. W. N. Hargreaves-Mawdsley. *Oxford in the Age of John Locke.*
33. Bonner Mitchell. *Rome in the High Renaissance: The Age of Leo X.*
34. William Spencer. *Algiers in the Age of Corsairs.*

35. Marilyn Stokstad. *Santiago de Compostela: In the Age of the Great Pilgrimages.*

UNIVERSITY OF OKLAHOMA PRESS

NORMAN